Understanding and Preventing Corruption

10.1057/9781137335098

Crime Prevention and Security Management

Series Editor: **Martin Gill**

Titles include:

Paul Almond
CORPORATE MANSLAUGHTER AND REGULATORY REFORM

Rachel Armitage
CRIME PREVENTION THROUGH HOUSING DESIGN
Policy and Practice

Joshua Bamfield
SHOPPING AND CRIME

Daniel Donnelly
MUNICIPAL POLICING IN THE EUROPEAN UNION
Comparative Perspectives

Paul Ekblom
CRIME PREVENTION, SECURITY AND COMMUNITY SAFETY USING THE 5IS FRAMEWORK

Adam Graycar and Tim Prenzler
UNDERSTANDING AND PREVENTING CORRUPTION

Bob Hoogenboom
THE GOVERNANCE OF POLICING AND SECURITY
Ironies, Myths and Paradoxes

Daniel McCarthy
'SOFT' POLICING
The Collaborative Control of Anti-Social Behaviour

Tim Prenzler
POLICING AND SECURITY IN PRACTICE
Challenges and Achievements

Emmeline Taylor
SURVEILLANCE SCHOOLS
Security, Discipline and Control in Contemporary Education

Jan van Dijk, AndromachiTseloni and Graham Farrell (*editors*)
THE INTERNATIONAL CRIME DROP
New Directions in Research

Adam White
THE POLITICS OF PRIVATE SECURITY
Regulation, Reform and Re-Legitimation

Crime Prevention and Security Management
Series Standing Order ISBN   978–0–230–01355–1 **hardback**
                 978–0–230–01356–8 **paperback**
(*outside North America only*)

You can receive future titles in this series as they are published by placing a standing order. Please contact your bookseller or, in case of difficulty, write to us at the address below with your name and address, the title of the series and one of the ISBNs quoted above.

Customer Services Department, Macmillan Distribution Ltd, Houndmills, Basingstoke, Hampshire RG21 6XS, England

10.1057/9781137335098

palgrave▸pivot

Understanding and Preventing Corruption

Adam Graycar
Professor of Public Policy, Australian National University

and

Tim Prenzler
Professor and Chief Investigator, Australian Research Council Centre of Excellence in Policing and Security, Griffith University, Australia

palgrave
macmillan

10.1057/9781137335098

First published 2013 by
PALGRAVE MACMILLAN

Palgrave Macmillan in the UK is an imprint of Macmillan Publishers Limited, registered in England, company number 785998, of Houndmills, Basingstoke, Hampshire RG21 6XS.

Palgrave Macmillan in the US is a division of St Martin's Press LLC, 175 Fifth Avenue, New York, NY 10010.

Palgrave Macmillan is the global academic imprint of the above companies and has companies and representatives throughout the world.

Palgrave® and Macmillan® are registered trademarks in the United States, the United Kingdom, Europe and other countries

ISBN: 978-1-137-33510-4 EPUB
ISBN: 978-1-137-33509-8 PDF
ISBN: 978-1-137-33508-1 Hardback

This book is printed on paper suitable for recycling and made from fully managed and sustained forest sources. Logging, pulping and manufacturing processes are expected to conform to the environmental regulations of the country of origin.

A catalogue record for this book is available from the British Library.

A catalog record for this book is available from the Library of Congress.

www.palgrave.com/pivot

DOI: 10.1057/9781137335098

Contents

List of Illustrations   vi

Preface   vii

Series Editor's Introduction   ix

Part I   Corruption Is Complex

1   Describing Corruption   2

2   Understanding Corruption   18

3   Measuring Corruption   33

Part II   Designing Counter-Measures

4   The Architecture of Corruption Control   50

5   Applying Crime Prevention and Regulatory
    Theory to Corruption   70

Part III   Combating and Reducing Corruption

6   Preventing Corruption in Criminal Justice   87

7   Preventing Corruption in Public Sector
    Procurement   100

8   Preventing Corruption in Public Health   114

9   Designing out Corruption in Urban Planning   127

Postscript   140

References   145

Index   156

List of Illustrations

Tables

1.1	Types, Activities, Sectors, Places (TASP): corrupt behaviours in four dispositions	11
1.2	Analytic pointers to corruption	15
2.1	A corruption checklist	30
3.1	Key features of measurement tool generations	36
3.2	Some corruption measures	46
4.1	Treaties and international arrangements	60
5.1	Police anti-corruption strategies containing a situational component	77
5.2	Opportunity-reducing techniques derived from theft findings	78

Figures

2.1	The pillars of integrity	31
3.1	Measuring corruption	41

10.1057/9781137335098

Preface

Corruption is a phenomenon about which many people have a view. In rich countries many see corruption as the mechanism by which scoundrel politicians and officials play their manipulative and self-serving games. Rich countries should get things right, the argument goes, because they have the resources to do so much. When they don't, one explanation for the failure is corruption, at all its levels and in all its forms. In poorer countries with limited resources, corruption is often blamed for failure to develop and deliver adequate human services, infrastructure and environmental assets or to derive revenues for the state from the extraction of natural resources.

While corruption has been part of politics forever, there is probably more debate about it now, more than a decade ago, more than a century ago, more than a millennium ago. Corruption, of course, is not limited to the political domain. There are many instances of damaging corruption in private sector activities. Corruption in private sector financial companies brought economic havoc to the world in recent years. Examples of corruption can be found in local and multinational companies, in the professions, in religious institutions, in non-profit organizations and, very notably, in the domain of sports.

To cover all of these types and contexts would need a book much larger than this one. The authors recognize the wide spectrum of corrupt activities, but this book focuses primarily on public sector corruption in rich countries.

The study of corruption often embeds itself within narrow academic boundaries, and thus we have excellent books and articles on corruption by philosophers, lawyers, sociologists, economists, psychologists, public administration scholars, historians, political scientists and development specialists. The methods they use and the literature they cite usually come from their own disciplines. Much of the literature is high powered, deeply analytical and is devoured by specialist audiences. Yet we are dealing with a phenomenon that cuts across many academic disciplines.

We saw the need for a general book that introduces readers to the study of corruption, a book that describes and classifies some aspects of corruption and lays out a basis for its prevention, however it is defined and however it manifests itself. In outlining preventive measures we draw on criminological theory, but overall we see this as a general book and not something aimed exclusively at a criminological readership.

For this short book we made judgements about what to cover, and this meant excluding many topics that are worthy of scrutiny. The book is a result of research that has been conducted over many years by the two authors. We are grateful to Caroline Compton, Matti Joutsen, John McFarlane, Denis Osborne and Elizabeth Percival, who read early drafts of some of the chapters. Their robust critical comments and wise advice are highly valued and gratefully appreciated.

10.1057/9781137335098

Series Editor's Introduction

Adam Graycar and Tim Prenzler's book offers an important insight into why and how corruption occurs and the key ways in which mitigation strategies can succeed and fail. The authors highlight how persistent and ubiquitous the problem of corruption is, across time and evident in all parts of the globe. They examine its various forms: the difference between petty and grand corruption and the distinction between what is a bribe and what constitutes a gift. They explain the meanings and implications of different forms of potentially corrupt behaviour including extortion (which may not be a crime), embezzlement, conflicts of interest, influence peddling, pay to play and different examples of favouritism such as patronage, nepotism and cronyism.

They discuss chillingly the range of consequences that can result in circumstances where corruption is allowed to take a grip. This is more than lost revenue (astronomical though that can be); through varied examples at different points in this book they point to the approval of inadequate infrastructure leading to buildings with fire and safety hazards; the entrance into the supply chain of counterfeit goods (e.g. drugs) including those that can kill; the reduction in impact of a variety of programmes including those for healthcare; the loss of amenities in local communities including in some cases water supply; in a different way to miscarriages of justice and to the undermining of democracy. In short the consequences are pernicious and can result in deaths.

While measuring corruption has long been recognized as a problem especially in poor countries where there is often inadequate data, in this text the authors outline the different methodologies used and criteria adopted with their various strengths and weaknesses. They chart the various factors that contribute to corruption in different systems using Max Weber's three 'authority systems' (traditional, patrimonial and rational–legal) as a framework. Rational Choice Theory has a relevance, so too Designing Out Crime approaches, but most attention is focussed on Ron Clarke's situational crime prevention framework and specifically opportunity reduction.

In practical terms the authors provide a checklist and various helpful categorizations to guide remedial action. They note the importance of political will in generating change, and the need for anti corruption approaches to be well thought through, targeted on specific problems, managed and implemented by capable people appropriately resourced for the task, with sufficient strategies at their disposal, and with proactive support from relevant stakeholders. For anyone wanting to understand corruption, and wanting to know how to understand and respond, this book will be an essential read.

Martin Gill
September 2013

10.1057/9781137335098

Part I
Corruption Is Complex

▶

10.1057/9781137335098

1
Describing Corruption

Abstract: *Rather than defining the term 'corruption', the opening chapter introduces the topic of corruption by firstly identifying types of behaviours typically labelled 'corruption', including bribery, extortion, embezzlement, conflicts of interest, patronage, nepotism and cronyism. The chapter also addresses the issue of grey areas, especially around customary gift giving. The focus then moves to the question of where corruption occurs by introducing the TASP model of analysis – Types, Activities, Sectors and Places. Diverse examples of corruption are provided across these domains. Attention is also given to the scale of corrupt activities in different locations, using a number of case studies, including examples of large-scale and endemic corruption.*

Graycar, Adam and Prenzler, Tim. *Understanding and Preventing Corruption.* Basingstoke: Palgrave Macmillan, 2013. DOI: 10.1057/9781137335098.

10.1057/9781137335098

Types of corruption

Corruption has been with us since the beginning of time. It is not a new phenomenon of the 21st century. There is probably no more corruption now than there was in ancient times, though it is hard to assemble the evidence to support this judgement. What we do know is that corruption causes both harm and outrage when it is discovered in modern industrial societies, and responding to it becomes a matter of significant debate and often government action.

Corruption in our world affects everybody. All countries experience corruption. The World Economic Forum (2013) has estimated that the cost of corruption equals more than 5 per cent of global GDP (about US$2.6 trillion). Corruption adds up to about 10 per cent of the total cost of doing business globally. The World Bank (2007) has estimated that about $1 trillion per year is paid in bribes, while about $40 billion per year is looted by corrupt political leaders. The impacts of corruption severely and disproportionally affect the poorest and most vulnerable in any society, and when it is widespread, corruption deters investment, weakens economic growth and undermines the basis for law and order. In rich countries corruption pushes taxes to higher levels than they need be, and reduces services to lesser quality than they might be.

Throughout history people have always sought to advance their position, get a better deal, make more money, or look after those near and dear to them. How they do this has been documented by anthropologists, economists, sociologists, political scientists, lawyers and many other scholars. Mostly such scholars record the accepted and legitimate processes by which these ends are achieved. This is the stuff of social sciences. However, there are times when these ends are gained by misuse of positions of power or of resources that are commonly owned. This is when corruption comes into play.

There are many behaviours that can be deemed corrupt. These occur in many settings, and have varying consequences. Very often there is debate about whether the behaviour is acceptable, harmful or simply routine.

Bribery, the most commonly perceived aspect of corrupt behaviour, occurs when somebody offers money to persuade another to do something that is wrong or, if not wrong, inappropriate in the circumstances. It is done to facilitate a satisfactory outcome that might not have happened without the money, or might not have happened as quickly. The

10.1057/9781137335098

inducement might be in cash, but it could also be in the form of inside information, meals and entertainment, holidays, employment, sexual favours. It can involve getting somebody to do something, not to do something, or to overlook something.

In return for money an official at a motor registry may allow somebody waiting in line for a long time to have their matter dealt with more quickly, or provide somebody with something to which they are not entitled, such as a driver's licence without having passed the correct test. In some countries doctors receive money to see patients more quickly (or at all!) or teachers to give students good results. Health inspectors may receive money to overlook unhygienic conditions in a restaurant kitchen, while judges may receive money to adjudicate in favour of the party offering the bribe.

Sometimes the bribe is very small and the stakes are low: for example, allowing somebody, for a few dollars, to jump the queue and have their matter dealt with quickly. Sometimes the stakes can be more serious, such as in allowing somebody without the necessary skills to be on the road, or to use equipment or to deliver services which could harm the public if not done correctly, or having a legal case settled corruptly with significant winners and losers.

Sometimes the stakes are much higher, and can affect companies or communities. A corrupt official can be bribed by a company to issue government contracts to that company. This can be for something minor such as ordering photocopier toner from a specific supplier, or more substantial such as ordering medical supplies for a hospital, all the way up to an entire health system, or buying planes under a huge defence contract. Sometimes it is just business, and one company wins the contract and another loses. At other times the consequences are severe, such as when bribery enables the erection of unsafe high-rise buildings, the illegal logging of environmentally pristine forest, or building dams and diverting water so that both communities and the environment suffer, while a corrupt official benefits.

As already noted, the payments are not always in cash. A gift of tickets to a regular sporting event can make the recipient act favourably towards the person offering the tickets. When it is a ticket to some major and highly desirable event the ticket can be particularly valuable, as might be the consideration in return. Lavish holidays may be offered by drug companies to doctors to persuade them to prescribe specific brands of drugs; developers wishing to undertake construction in contravention

10.1057/9781137335098

of a building code may offer municipal officers free renovations or other building work on their homes, or a municipal officer regulating brothels may be offered 'free' sex.

Bribery can involve large amounts of money or small amounts, or no cash at all. It can be for something minor, or its results can have profound consequences. It can flow in either direction. It can be offered by the principal, or it can be solicited by the agent. There are many terms in many cultures which describe bribery – kickbacks, sweetheart deals, baksheesh, payola, secret commissions, incentive payments, perks, gratuities, fringe benefits, and 'a drink for you', to mention just a few.

Extortion involves the use of force or threat or intimidation to extract payments. Coercion is the key here, but it need not necessarily be physical. A health inspector who threatens to shut down a restaurant even though all is in order, and a safety inspector who threatens to shut down a building site if a payment is not made, are practising extortion, as is a court official who will 'lose' a file and delay or prejudice a case if a payment is not made. Again, it is not always cash that is extorted. Teachers have sought sex from students in return for good results; employers have sought sex from job seekers to obtain a job, or from employees to keep the job. A customs official may want a share of goods brought into a country illicitly, or a police officer a share of drugs that are being seized.

Again, there is a matter of scale and impact in the extortion. A few dollars for a health inspector threatening to report a clean kitchen as dirty, or a police officer seeking money or else s/he will book you for speeding, are different from an official withholding approval for a major construction, a customs official refusing to clear a shipload of bananas that will rot in the sun unless the paperwork is done, or a group of stevedores refusing to unload these bananas. Corrupt tax officials may extort and intimidate while armed police or military, or unarmed border officials, may extort to allow one to pass through a checkpoint. Organized crime has a long history of both corruption and extortion, and at times combines both to achieve results.

Misappropriation, theft, fraud or *embezzlement* can be corrupt. While certainly criminal, most examples of theft do not involve corruption. Shoplifting, burglary, stealing from the boss, writing dud cheques or robbing a bank are not acts of corruption. A government official who steals money from the safe at work is not involved in government corruption. S/he is a thief.

10.1057/9781137335098

When one uses one's office or position to steal that for which one has responsibility, then theft and fraud have a place in corruption studies. The scale can be huge, such as when political leaders stash some of their nation's money in personal foreign bank accounts. Or it can involve an official selling food from a relief-aid shipment, or medical supplies that find their way into private practice when they have been donated for community health programmes. Officials who manipulate records or accounts so that a proportion of payments come to them are guilty of corrupt misappropriation. All sorts of contract manipulation and pro- curement irregularities come into play here. Where misappropriation is part of the corruption lexicon it takes away funds from public sources, and the consequence is that policy goals of government cannot be achieved, or services to help citizens are diminished.

Self-dealing involves taking advantage of one's position in order to fur- ther one's interests rather than the interests of the organization. It may involve hiring one's own company or the company belonging to close associates or relatives to provide public services, and avoiding tender processes. In this way the organization does not necessarily receive the best-priced or best-delivered services. Examples include the head of maintenance at a public university who issued cleaning contracts to a company owned by her and her husband, and excluded other competi- tion, and a purchasing officer who owned a share in a car dealership and who would purchase official vehicles only from that dealership. In one suburban municipality it was necessary to obtain a certificate from the council before a house could be sold (to show that there had been no unauthorized alterations or renovations). The mayor's family owned one of the real estate companies in town, and from time to time a certificate would not be forthcoming unless the property was listed with the mayor's family company. Canadian political scientists Kernaghan and Langford (1990) define self-dealing as 'a situation where one takes an action in an official capacity which involves dealing with oneself in a private capacity and which confers a benefit on oneself'. Self-dealing is essentially a form of conflict of interest.

Conflict of interest occurs when an individual occupying a formal posi- tion is required to make (public) decisions, but a decision made in a cer- tain way might benefit that individual privately. Conflict of interest does not necessarily involve cash: it might entail the possibility of promoting a cause about which the individual cares or placing somebody near and dear into a favourable position. In essence the individual is acting neither

10.1057/9781137335098

independently nor objectively when that is expected of him or her, and the decision which puts private benefit ahead of professional judgement is one based on conflict of interest. An advertising agency could not (ethically) represent two companies that had products that were in competition with each other, and a lawyer would not represent a client while at the same time representing a client with conflicting interests.

Conflict of interest occurs often in politics. Politicians have many interests paraded before them and thrust upon them, and support and resolution may at times appear conflicted. There may be no improper act in a discussion or a decision, but perception is also a very important part of the integrity structure. Gifts are sometimes given to officials by people or organizations about whom the official must make professional decisions, and the acceptance of gifts signals at least a potential conflict.

Politicians represent interests, and one might expect that they would be in sympathy with the interests they represent. For this reason a line has to be drawn between the general interests of the community that they represent and what they believe is best for the whole community, and the special interests that may wish to seek advantage. Lobbyists seek the best outcomes for their clients, and politicians, one would expect, seek the best outcomes for their communities. Campaign donations may distort a politician's or party's interest.

Egregious examples of conflict of interest have occurred in business. During the global financial crisis of 2008 certain American financial organizations were marketing mortgage-backed securities to their clients, telling them they were a good investment, while at the same time investing in insurance products that would pay handsomely if the securities failed. In essence there was a conflict of interest in persuading clients to invest in toxic securities which if they failed (and they were likely to do so) would yield significant financial benefit to the seller. The large energy company Enron exhibited destructive conflict of interest when it created an electricity shortage in California in June 2000 in order to boost the price of its product. The company caused massive damage to consumers, businesses and communities in order to maximize profits, while it had a clear obligation to ensure a safe and affordable electricity supply (McLean & Elkind, 2004).

Exploiting conflicts of interest creates many problems, and is also the subject of a great deal of debate, since different standards are often brought to bear. Conflict of interest is usually problematic behaviour that crosses a boundary, though judgements of where that boundary lies

10.1057/9781137335098

vary. While those with conflicts should certainly make full disclosure, or recuse themselves from relevant discussions and decisions, it is best if situations are structured so that the conflict does not arise at all.

Abuse of discretion is very common. Without discretion the wheels of government and business would grind excruciatingly slowly. Routine decisions have to be made about everyday but important issues such as the issuing of permits and licences, procurement, real estate developments, entry of goods and people at the border, treatment for sick people, planning of transport routes, safety in the workplace, and so on.

Abuse of discretion occurs when somebody exceeds their legal boundaries. They may do so for a consideration (a bribe, as described above), or they may extort (as also described above) in exercising their discretion. For example, if an official makes judgements about competencies to drive and obtain a driver's licence, discretion is abused if that official grants the licence because somebody has offered an inducement, or because he or she thinks the person deserves it even if their driving is not good enough, or because the official thinks that this person is charming, amusing or attractive.

Patronage occurs when a wealthy or powerful person sponsors another in employment or promotes them to an influential position, favouring them over more qualified candidates. The person so promoted becomes obligated to the patron who, in turn, may wish to seek influence, wealth, status or power. By circumventing the normal merit processes a patron can corruptly distort a transparent process and diminish integrity in decision making.

Patronage in the arts is a long-standing activity, and central to the way the arts have always flourished. Patronage in politics is tied up with genuine electoral interests, and leaders elected democratically are entitled to have in their teams people of similar ideological and other values. What is important here is that the boundaries are clear and that there is transparency in processes. Patronage is the glue that holds many tribal societies together; structures, relationships and patronage are explained at length in the anthropological literature.

Nepotism, the inappropriate provision of benefits to family and friends, is corrupt behaviour. In a modern society when people are favoured because they are related to a person in power, the demonstration of partiality and preferential treatment undermines many proper processes. If people get positions in public life or opportunities because of who they are rather than what they are capable of doing, then the merit principle

10.1057/9781137335098

that underpins good governance is undermined, and good governance suffers; those who lose out will feel cheated and resentful and that can be dangerous.

Those obtaining positions because of who they know may expect promotion for the same reason, and have no incentive to work hard, thus demoralizing other staff. By contrast, nepotism on the family farm or in the family law business is legal and a family member appointed there has every incentive to work well. If they don't, they will be in disgrace with the family; if they do they can hope for a share in the profits.

In many countries politicians have placed their relatives in public positions or in situations where they have access to business interests from which they can benefit financially, which would not be available if their relative was not in power. This can distort public policy and cause harm. Nepotism has been part of human behaviour throughout history and is examined extensively in the anthropological literature, since it is common in all societies for people to favour their family members.

Cronyism is similar to nepotism, but rather than the beneficiary being a family member it is a friend, acquaintance or business associate who obtains benefits. Patronage, nepotism and cronyism are examples of favouritism in which who you are, rather than what you can do, is the criterion for bestowing benefits.

Trading in influence or *influence peddling* occurs in many public transactions, and is at the margins of corrupt behaviour. There are times when blatant displays of one's connections with people in power are sold. That is, if the agent is well connected, then for a fee one can get connections, benefits and results. This can be used to obtain power or money. Former Governor of Illinois Rod Blagojevich was imprisoned for 14 years in 2012 for ostensibly offering to sell the senate seat vacated by Barack Obama, but was accused of a much wider range of influence peddling in which he wheeled and dealed and used state resources and state offices as playthings and bargaining chips. However, influence peddling is not necessarily illegal. In some circumstances it is part of the regular business of politics, but in others it crosses a legal boundary.

'*Pay to play*' is part of many systems. It describes a situation where one has to pay money to be a player: that is, to be able to receive contracts, or even be allowed to bid for contracts. In politics the common means is for an entity (a person, corporation or other organization) to make a campaign contribution and, in return, be awarded a no-bid contract, government funding or favourable legislation.

10.1057/9781137335098

Where is corruption found? (TASP)

Corruption occurs in political regimes, organizations of every type, businesses and institutions such as schools, hospitals, police forces. Two things need to be noted. First, some of the behaviours described above are nearly always criminal, such as bribery and theft. All nations have statutes that criminalize the payment of bribes, and there are international agreements that make it unlawful in most developed countries to bribe a foreign official.

Extortion, on the other hand, is not necessarily a crime. Companies that price-gouge and people who charge excessively for specialized services may well be accused of extortion, but they have not necessarily broken laws, and would defend their situation as opportunistic business practice. A professional or an employer seeking sex from a client or an employee is behaving highly unethically, but may or may not have broken a law. Conflict of interest usually does not breach laws, but creates issues of ethics and perceptions. Second, these behaviours can occur in a variety of settings, and every activity has its own defining characteristics.

What is notable in respect of this point is that there is no single definition of corruption. Many academic publications work laboriously through definitions and nuances, and many pieces of legislation have complex and convoluted legal definitions. The United Nations Convention against Corruption, the most comprehensive anti-corruption instrument that exists, does not attempt a definition. Rather it assumes that people dealing with corruption will know what they are dealing with. The same principle applies in this book, although as a general working guide, the definition of corruption used by Transparency International (2010), 'the abuse of entrusted power for private gain', will be used to describe the activities covered here.

Rather than seeking a tight definition of corruption, this book instead works on the premise that corruption comprises a variety of behaviours or types, such as those listed above. It occurs in different settings, and in different places. Understanding these will help develop mechanisms to counter these activities which undermine many principles of good governance.

Corruption may occur in different types of *activities*: personnel management, hiring and firing people; buying things (procurement); delivering programmes or services; making things (construction/manufacturing); controlling activities (licensing/regulation/issuing of permits); and administration (of justice, for example). This list is by no means exhaustive, and other activities can be added.

By the same token, corruption occurs in many *sectors* in our society. Often it is found in government, business, access to information, sporting activities, the legal system, the humanitarian aid system and so on. Sometimes the sector crosses government, private sector and non-profit. In the health sector, for example, government health policies can be corrupted; private corporate suppliers of equipment and drugs can be involved in bribery or self-dealing; professionals can withhold services or misappropriate equipment; and NGOs charged with the delivery of primary health services can divert the benefits, be cheated out of supplies or have their priorities rearranged by corrupt officials. It is certainly a complex web.

If we look at government activities we could draw up a list of sectors that would include construction, health, tax administration, defence, energy, environment and water, forestry, border control, customs and immigration, welfare systems, the legal system, agriculture, urban planning and so on.

To round off, we can identify *places* where corruption can occur: countries, regions, localities or workplaces.

This classification can be used to break corrupt events into analytical units by identifying the Types, Activities, Sectors and Places (TASP) (see Table 1.1). For example, we might be able to identify an act that involves

TABLE 1.1   *Types, Activities, Sectors, Places (TASP): corrupt behaviours in four dispositions*

Types	Activities	Sectors	Places
• Bribery	• Appointing personnel	• Construction	• Countries
• Extortion	• Buying things	• Health	• Regions
• Misappropriation	(procurement)	• Tax administration	• Localities
• Self-dealing	• Delivering	• Energy	• Workplaces
• Conflict of interest	programmes or	• Environment and water	• etc.
• Abuse of discretion	services	• Forestry	
• Patronage	• Making things	• Customs and	
• Nepotism,	(construction/	immigration	
• Cronyism	manufacturing)	• Welfare systems	
• Trading in influence	• Controlling activities	• Agriculture	
• Pay to play	(licensing/regulation/	• Urban planning	
• etc.	issuing of permits)	• Legal system	
	• Administering	• etc	
	(justice, for		
	example) etc		

10.1057/9781137335098

bribery in controlling activities (issuing of permits to log) in the forestry sector in a region. Or there might be abuse of discretion in delivering programmes in the welfare sector in one particular office, or there might be nepotism in appointing personnel in the urban planning sector in a municipality. This level of analysis helps place corruption in a context and enables planning how remedial action might be undertaken.

Corruption, minor and mega

It is important also to get a sense of the scale of any corrupt activity. Much corrupt activity involves relatively small amounts of money changing hands to obtain some basic service or a permit, or to prevent something like a small fine or a parking or speeding ticket. It also covers lots of contracts and purchases in municipal activities, aid programmes, bribes for medical or educational services, purchase of textbooks in educational programmes. Although the consequences can be severe, this type of corruption is often termed *petty corruption*.

This contrasts with *grand corruption* where the state becomes the plaything of its leaders. This form of corruption involves those at the highest level of government, who loot the Treasury and improperly and dishonestly manipulate and control the institutions of power.

Alfredo Stroessner was President of Paraguay for 35 years until 1989. He manipulated just about every aspect of state activity, disposing of public resources as if they were his property. He took kickbacks on all sorts of contracts and construction, as well as running drugs and laundering money through his banks. As a public official he put billions of state dollars into his personal bank accounts (Gunson, 2006).

Mobutu Sese Seko was President of Zaire (now the Democratic Republic of the Congo) for 33 years until 1997. One-third of the state budget was under his personal control. He amassed vast personal wealth, controlled the copper trade and siphoned off a large part of the profits which he shared with his cronies (Kiley, 1997).

President Suharto of Indonesia was reputed to have looted up to $35 billion through a complex network of family businesses and nepotism, cronyism, and every sort of corrupt activity in most government sectors (Terrall, 2008).

One could list many leaders who amassed vast personal fortunes while in government, such as Ferdinand Marcos in the Philippines, Muammar

10.1057/9781137335098

Gaddafi in Libya and Arnoldo Alemán of Nicaragua. South Korean Presidents Roh Tae-woo and Chun Doo-hwan received large pay-offs and, later, long prison sentences. Former Taiwanese President Chen Shui-Ban and his wife were sentenced to life for complex corruption issues involving, for example, government contracts.

These rulers have been alleged to be manipulators and fixers – manipulating every aspect of government, dispensing favours, shaping taxes and concessions, setting the regulatory framework to suit their own interests and enriching themselves at the expense of the poor in their countries.

Sometimes petty corruption and grand corruption come together and explode in mass outrage, as happened in the Arab Spring in early 2011. Several regimes fell following activities as diverse as poor street vendors being shaken down by corrupt local officials in Tunisia, and Presidents Hosni Mubarak of Egypt and Muammar Gaddafi of Libya being accused of grand corruption.

Another form of corruption on a grand scale and with huge consequences is known as *state capture*. Rather than officials shaking down citizens or kleptocrats dominating business and stealing the country's assets, situations arise where legislation, formally developed and properly passed by the legislature or parliament, grants benefits in a corrupt manner. Outside interests not only bend state laws, but use their corrupt influence to have laws written for them. Powerful interests can influence or bribe officials and parliamentarians to write legislation that might give a company access to the exploitation of natural resources, a monopoly on a railway line or exemption from the payment of taxes.

In transitional economies there is great vulnerability to state capture. In Russia, as the economy transitioned from communism to capitalism during the 1990s, many state enterprises were privatized. In many cases favours were exchanged for such assets. Factories were privatized and some state assets were disposed off corruptly, though with formal legislation. Oil and gas exploration and transmission were expanded, and huge investments were made in pipelines and transport arrangements. Legislation was written to grant exclusivity, set tax rates and establish regulatory arrangements. Politicians who wrote the legislation were rewarded handsomely. Sometimes they were made company directors and received regular income flows, but overall they sold their legislative integrity (Yakovlev & Zhuravskaya, 2006).

It is not only in transitional economies that there is state capture. There is a fine line between lobbying in a democratic system where, on behalf

10.1057/9781137335098

of companies or industry associations, lobbyists seek to have legislation written to favour their activities. Sometimes this is done corruptly with payments of cash, sometimes with gifts, sometimes subtly with contributions to political campaigns, or by donations to causes supported by the politician.

Malcolm Salter (2010) describes how the gaming of society's rules by corporations contributes to the problem of institutional corruption in the world of business. 'Gaming' in its various forms involves the use of technically legal means to subvert the intent of society's rules in order to gain advantage. Salter refers to one form of gaming, which he calls the Rule-Making Game. This involves influencing the writing of society's rules by legislative or regulatory bodies, so that loopholes, exclusions and ambiguous language provide future opportunities to 'work around' or circumvent the intent of the rules for private gain. The Rule-Making Game is an influence game that occurs in all democratic societies.

Harvard law professor Lawrence Lessig (2011) analyses the complexity of American policy making and argues that there are two types of corruption. The first type is that which is described in this chapter: bribery, extortion, misappropriation, nepotism and so on. What he calls Type Two corruption is the dependence that legislators have on campaign donors and other stakeholders. The billions of dollars that come to US congress members and senators do not normally come with strict and specific strings attached, though there are cases when powerful interests are clearly favoured. There is a more insidious situation of congressmen not wanting to support policies or programmes that might upset their donors. This dependency on campaign funds and alignment with interests distorts the process, but there is no clear personal dollar gain for the congressmen, other than furthering their career. In essence, Lessig argues (p. 234) that it is not just the bad people who effect corruption, but the institutions that make it possible.

Jack Abramoff is a former Washington lobbyist who received a six-year sentence for conspiracy to bribe public officials. Following his release from federal prison, he wrote about the new corruption. 'No one', he said, 'would seriously propose visiting a judge before a trial and offering a financial gratuity, or choice tickets to an athletic event, in exchange for special consideration from the bench'. Yet, he observes, nobody minds 'when a congressman receives a campaign contribution even as he contemplates action on an issue of vital importance to the donor'. He notes pertinently: 'When a public servant has a debt to someone seeking a favour from the government, the foundation of our government is at risk. Each time a lobbyist or special interest makes a political contribution to a public servant, a debt is created. Lobbyists are very adept at collecting these debts' (Abramoff, 2012).

Pulling some threads together

In simplistic terms corruption may be driven by *need*, or maybe by *greed*. Sometimes it is claimed that officials, usually in poor countries, receive such low salaries that they need to extort to survive. At the other end of the spectrum, greed is a powerful driver of human behaviour that shapes a lot of corrupt activity. Any analysis of corruption should seek to make judgements of the drivers, though this is not always possible without in-depth investigation of motive.

Any analysis of corruption should explore where the corruption is actually located. Are we analysing the behaviour of corrupt *individuals*, corrupt *organizations* or corrupt *societies*?

When an individual is deemed to be corrupt, it is often said that there is a rotten apple in the barrel. If this is so, precipitating causes and opportunities can be examined, and action taken against the individual. It is important that individuals are not able to exploit the structural matters that gave rise to the corruption. Integrity in individual behaviour, adherence to procedures and professionalism are some of the foundations for limiting individual corruption.

Certainly there are organizations in which corruption is rife. In these cases there is an abandonment of the goals of the organization, and a lack of ethical behaviour. Corrupt organizations have a culture of failing to do what they are required to do, implementing policy inappropriately or simply doing wrong things. The huge energy company Enron was universally deemed to be a corrupt organization (though not all the employees, by any means, were corrupt or indulged in corrupt behaviour).

TABLE 1.2   *Analytic pointers to corruption*

Corrupt events occur in / are perpetrated by

- Corrupt societies
- Corrupt organizations
- Corrupt individuals

Different controls apply

Between 2001 and 2007, Siemens, the German multinational with a wide range of businesses across the globe, made some 4,283 corrupt payments to foreign officials totalling over $US 1.4 billion. Up until 1999 in Germany corrupt payments to foreign officials were tax-deductible expenses. This led to the systematic embedding of a bribery culture within the organization, which included management instructions on how to set up shell companies in order to funnel illicit payments to foreign officials. As a corrupt organization Siemens was indicted and prosecuted in Germany, the USA and Italy (see http://www.fcpablog.com/blog/tag/siemens?currentPage=8). Overall their breaches of procurement policies cost the company $2.6 billion–$1.6 billion in fines in Germany and the USA, and $1 billion in self-initiated corporate reforms.

In past decades organizations as diverse as the Indonesian army, the New York Police Department and the Queensland (Australia) police force were regarded at times as being corrupt organizations, as was the company that ran the railways in New South Wales, Australia, RailCorp.

In 2008 the NSW Independent Commission against Corruption (ICAC NSW) released eight reports documenting endemic and enduring corruption in RailCorp which involved employees and managers at many levels of the organization. The Commission investigated allegations of fraud, bribery, improper allocation of contracts, unauthorized secondary employment, failure to declare conflicts of interest, falsification of timesheets and the cover-up of a safety breach. In financial terms RailCorp employees were found to have improperly allocated contracts totalling almost $19 million to companies owned by themselves, their friends or their families, in return for corrupt payments totalling over $2.5 million. This investigation exposed an extraordinary extent of public sector corruption. Corrupt employees appeared to be confident that they would not be caught or if they were, that not much would happen to them.

Sometimes whole societies are deemed corrupt. In some countries corruption pervades every aspect of life. At the bottom end bribes are required for every public service, such as education, health services or to obtain a licence to sell vegetables. In government and business, cronyism and nepotism are rife, while red tape strangles most transactions. At the top end, leaders use the state for their own indulgence and enrich themselves by making bad laws and approving and having a share of developments that are not in the interests of the people or the environment. Often money is stashed away in foreign bank accounts while the poor suffer terribly (Wrong, 2009).

10.1057/9781137335098

It is not, however, just poor countries where society is corrupt. In Italy, for example, it is customary for favours to be exchanged; getting a job in the civil service or municipal government depends on who you know rather than what you can do, and contracts are awarded in a less than transparent manner (Della Porta & Vannucci, 1999).

To this point we can see that corruption is not a single concept, and might find its manifestation in different types of behaviour, activities, sectors, places. It might be driven by need or greed, could be grand or petty, or involve state capture. There might be corrupt individuals, corrupt organizations or corrupt societies, or any combinations of these. Moving forward, one useful way of analysing corruption is to focus on corrupt *events*. If we use the event as the unit of analysis, then other analytic questions can help us shape our understanding of corruption and help propose responses.

10.1057/9781137335098

2

Understanding Corruption

Abstract: *The chapter begins by considering the function of corruption in three types of societies: 'traditional', 'patrimonial' and 'rational–legal'. Focusing on the highly variable nature of corruption, attention is then given to factors that facilitate corruption and factors that impede corruption. Frustration with government regulations can motivate many people to seek to engage in 'rent seeking' or obtaining monopoly control over an area of economic activity. Decision makers in government are also vulnerable to rent seeking in exploiting their control of an area of public demand, such as licences or approvals. The harmful effects of these types of practices are considered, especially in terms of the diminution of government services. Noting that different types of societies provide different opportunities for corruption, this chapter then examines the strategic role of key groups, in different types of societies and outlines specific opportunity factors in corruption, especially in transactions in government processes.*

Graycar, Adam and Prenzler, Tim. *Understanding and Preventing Corruption*. Basingstoke: Palgrave Macmillan, 2013. DOI: 10.1057/9781137335098.

10.1057/9781137335098

The previous chapter made the case that corruption takes many forms, and occurs in different settings. The way forward is to break the concept into small manageable pieces. The first task is to identify corrupt events and unpack them, subdividing them into components that identify type, activities, sectors and places. Of equal importance is to identify the nature of corrupt events and locate them in a socio-political and historical framework. The unit of analysis should be the corrupt event.

It is so often said that corruption has been part of history and nothing can be done about it. While the former is true, the latter is not. In recent years there have been many examples of countries becoming less corrupt, ethical standards being raised in organizations, and codes of personal behaviour being willingly accepted or, if not, vigorously implemented.

Some people are more corrupt than others, some places are more corrupt than others and some aspects of corruption are easier to tackle than others. Before working out what one might do about this, we need to dive more deeply into the murky waters.

Corruption in cultural context

The noted criminologist Marcus Felson (2011) observes that corruption is a product of the interplay between primary human needs and an economic and social system trying to control and channel those needs. He takes us back to the great social scientist Max Weber who saw, over the broad sweep of history, three 'authority systems': traditional, patrimonial and rational–legal.

Everyone living in traditional societies knows where they stand. Class, status and obligation are strongly entrenched and very rarely violated. The boundaries are pretty firm. In a patrimonial society, in turn, personal rule is the order, and the ruler does not distinguish between personal and public life, treating state resources and decisions as his or her personal affair. In a way we could say there was no corruption as we now know it in either traditional or patrimonial societies, since the nature of governance, without a scintilla of fairness, structures the nature of authority, and all understand their place. The rich, well born and well placed all have a good life, while the poor have a miserable life and are exploited. However, the exploitative behaviour, the lack of adherence to the rule of law, and the rent seeking (see page 21) do not count as corruption. That is part of traditional and patrimonial society!

10.1057/9781137335098

The rational–legal system is closely related to Weber's textbook concept of 'formal organization' and bureaucracy – a word he uses in a positive sense. Under this system, all persons follow rules and fit into formal roles that are separate from the personal, family and friendship interests of their incumbents (Felson, 2011, p. 13). Felson, however, notes that 'the rational-legal system of economic and social organization has an entirely different set of expectations from the traditional and patrimonial systems'.

A rational–legal system creates a fundamental tension in society, Felson notes, because it is only natural for each person to take care of oneself and one's family and friends, even in violation of general rules and roles. Indeed, corruption has much greater potential in the rational–legal system than in the traditional or patrimonial systems of economic and social organization. In a rational–legal system, attempts to seek self-interest often involve the breaking of rules, and the behaviour that underpins this is corrupt or criminal. In earlier types of society, seeking self-interest did not break rules, and therefore was not necessarily legally or technically corrupt as the unfairness was broadly accepted.

In modern societies, when personal interest drives a public official more than public service – that is, when personal benefits or advantage are put above the interests of those citizens that are to be served – a situation of corruption exists. For this to happen, formal rules and processes are replaced by informal processes. The institutions of society that require formal processes are undermined by informal processes that involve deals, bribery, nepotism, extortion, self-dealing, abuse of discretion, and all the behaviours listed in the previous chapter.

There is a theoretical tension in studying and responding to corruption. While not all corruption is the same, there is also debate about the causes and remedies. An examination of corruption in the broad sweep of history demonstrates that what counts as corruption now may not have been perceived as corruption in different times and places. An interesting analysis has been presented by Eric Uslaner in his book *Corruption, Inequality and the Rule of Law* (2008) where he posits an 'inequality trap' in which inequality leads to low trust which leads to corruption, which in turn leads to more inequality. While he undertakes a complex statistical analysis of correlates of corruption in different settings, the simple argument is that unequal distribution of resources makes any attempts to reduce corruption particularly fragile.

Changes in political institutions and other specific measures will not make much impact if inequality is pervasive. Uslaner relates the tale of an American political boss, 90 years ago, whose constituents were poor immigrants who often found themselves bewildered by the law, and often in all sorts of trouble. They could not afford lawyers, but came to him to (corruptly) fix things. He had a commodity that others did not – the ability to intervene. He was a patron, they were clients, and the corruption of the leaders was their fee for providing services to the poor. Economic inequality creates political leaders who 'take care' of constituents and make patronage a virtue rather than a vice (Uslaner, 2008, pp. 23–24). A culture of corruption, he says, emerges in impoverished settings and is part of an inequality trap, which is the underlying argument of his book.

This is all the more apposite in poor countries where efforts to clean up government do not always translate into less corruption because the fundamentals of inequality have not been eradicated. The perpetual and controversial argument about whether poverty causes corruption or corruption causes poverty continues to rage (see Khan & Kaufmann, 2009).

Uslaner claims that inequality, low trust and corruption form a vicious cycle and each persists over time. He argues that corruption leads to less effective government, while effective government does not necessarily lead to less corruption, more trust or less inequality (p. 30). Meanwhile, it has been suggested (in personal correspondence) that in many African countries the rich are more corrupt than the poor.

Gift giving and rent seeking

Cultures determine the acceptability of different types of behaviours. Giving substantial gifts to officials is frowned upon in most modern democracies, but throughout history gift giving has been a feature of social life. In many societies, a gift is a mark of respect to leadership. We are all familiar with situations in families and among friends when gift giving is more related to affection than obligation. The anthropologist Marcel Mauss (1950), however, argued that gift giving is a form of reciprocity and exchange is one of the processes that integrates a society. It is steeped in morality, since in giving, receiving and returning gifts a moral bond forms between those involved. What is of relevance to the study of corruption is the obligation that the receiving of a gift entails. As Mauss observed, there is a competitive and strategic aspect of gift giving. Like all issues in corruption, there are boundaries that separate behaviour that is deemed acceptable from that which is deemed unacceptable.

10.1057/9781137335098

In China, *guanxi* is a cultural set of arrangements where connections turn into favours and obligations. *Guanxi* literally means relationships. Those in a network congregate together and support one another. The networks of contacts and influence get things done and provide favours through social connections gained from family, workmates, school friends, business acquaintances and so on. *Guanxi* thus by definition bypasses formal tender or merit processes, but Chinese would be horrified to think of it as corruption because it is so deeply culturally embedded. Similar concepts of gift, obligation and reciprocity are present in many cultures, as are structured networks of influence and favours.

For many international businesspeople gifts are an important part of doing business. It is important to know what sort of gift is appropriate, since a gift that is too small will offend, as will one that is too large. However, most western countries have laws which make it an offence to bribe a foreign government official.

When is a gift a bribe, and when is it a normal part of human interaction? This depends on the nature of the obligation entailed. What is the intent of the gift? What is expected in return? Is the giving of the gift transparent? Is there anything to hide in the process? And is it a rent-seeking activity?

Rent seeking occurs when one tries to obtain monopoly privileges stemming from government regulation of a market. Those in public service are paid a salary to make decisions and implement policies. Sometimes they control scarce resources, such as the issuing of a licence, and they might not issue it without a bribe. This is rent seeking. They have a monopoly, they receive a salary for doing their job and their seeking a bribe does not add value nor increase productivity.

As Robert Klitgaard (1988) has noted, in a rent-seeking society citizens and officials strive to obtain monopoly rents, often through bribes. Speed money, by which civil servants speed up a process, may appear to add to efficiency, but as Klitgaard has observed, speed money has often led government officials to extort payments for the provision of any service at all. This rent-seeking behaviour, the tips and the speed money, then becomes the standard for required payments, and this leads to significant inefficiencies (Klitgaard, 1988, p. 41). When rent seeking exists, no wealth is created, and resources are obtained without adding value.

Susan Rose-Ackerman (1999, pp. 42–44) describes rent seeking which has occurred in the privatization of government assets, and also describes the downsides of rent seeking in natural-resources exploitation

10.1057/9781137335098

in countries rich in oil, minerals or diamonds. The existence of these resources does not necessarily promote economic development, since rent-seeking activities can help sustain corrupt regimes and often crowd out productive investment (1999, pp. 213–215).

Corruption harms

Both Rose-Ackerman and Klitgaard make the case persuasively that corruption is a harmful activity in both developing and developed countries, the damage it causes outweighing whatever social benefits are sometimes claimed. In a seminal paper Joseph Nye (1967) documented three downsides of corruption:

- ▶ its detrimental effects on economic development;
- ▶ its detrimental effects on national integration; and
- ▶ diminution of government capacity.

A recent study of municipal corruption in New York City that explored many corrupt events found results backing Nye's observations on diminution of government capacity (Graycar & Villa, 2011). The study examined 100 cases of mostly small-scale corruption. Examples included four building contractors who paid $500 to an inspector to overlook several building-code violations related to scaffolding safety issues; an employee of the City Department of Parks and Recreation who received $120 from a person obligated to perform community service as a part of an alternative sentence programme, to certify that the person performed the obligation, when in fact they did not turn up; a city water-use inspector who solicited and received bribes of between $100 and $250 for overlooking water-use violations which would have led to stiff fines and required remedial action; a drug-test technician responsible for collecting urine samples as part of pre-employment testing of such job applicants as truck drivers and maintenance workers, who accepted a $100 bribe to alter results; a plumbing inspector employed with the New York City Department of Buildings, who solicited and accepted a $500 bribe from a plumbing contractor in exchange for filing false certificates of inspection and falsely claiming that he had performed mandated inspections on two residential sewer connections.

What is notable about these cases is that the loss to the city of the corrupt behaviour was mostly a *loss of governance capacity*. The loss to the

10.1057/9781137335098

city was usually not a monetary loss, but rather an inability to deliver the protections, appropriate under laws and regulations, required for its citizens. In 81 per cent of the cases examined the loss to the city was one of governance capacity, while in 19 per cent of the cases the loss was monetary (Graycar & Villa, 2011). One example of the latter was a woman who fabricated false adoption cases, authorizing undue payments for a total of $411,775, in exchange for receiving a portion of that money.

These sorts of examples, certainly those concerning inspectors seeking small bribes to overlook infractions and violations, would not cause a ripple in most countries which have formidable development challenges, let alone the instigation of a process of enforcement, investigation and sanction. The consequences, however, can be delayed and disastrous, as we have seen when buildings collapse in earthquakes or hurricanes having been built with inferior products or poor workmanship after an inspector had been bribed for approval.

Corruption in political context

In theorizing corruption it is important to understand how the nature of a society's corruption fits into socio-economic and political development. Michael Johnston (2005, ch. 3) has identified a set of patterns or syndromes of corruption. He calls these

- ▶ Official moguls;
- ▶ Oligarchs and clans;
- ▶ Elite cartels; and
- ▶ Influence markets.

Official moguls dominate in weak undemocratic states where leaders use state power for personal use. They manipulate the economy and trash investment and aid inflows. Countries such as Pakistan, Sierra Leone, Zimbabwe, and Egypt until 2011 characterize this syndrome, though it should be noted that regime change occurs frequently in such countries and patterns can change.

Oligarchs and clans dominate in weak transitional regimes undergoing liberalization, where in the search for new markets, politics and the economy are opening up and opportunists are moving in to get part of the action. Countries such as Kenya, Turkey, Thailand and Bulgaria fit the bill here.

10.1057/9781137335098

Elite cartels hold both economic and political power and run things through networks of influence and personal connection. Even though the economy might be liberalized there is resistance to new participants and the sharing of wealth and influence. Corruption is fairly widespread, but tightly controlled by elites. This describes the situation in countries such as Italy, Taiwan, Greece and Argentina, for example.

In the first two of these syndromes economic institutions are weak, as is the capacity of the political institutions to provide ethical regulatory outcomes. In the third, elite cartels, the institutions, both economic and political, are moderately strong.

Influence markets is the syndrome of most interest in this book as it characterizes mature democratic states. We have seen that corruption certainly exists, but it is of a different nature, and the things deemed corrupt in these states could be brushed off as trivial in many other countries. Where economic institutions are strong and social and political capacity is robust, corruption is characterized by trading in influence. The activities and mechanisms that oil the process are political contributions, corporate corruption, purchase of access to politicians and bureaucrats, lobbying activities to 'game the system' and protect vested interests, and bought or contrived flexibility in the implementation of policies.

Finland is a country regarded as one of the least corrupt in the world (Transparency International, 2012). A recent analysis by the Finnish Ministry of Justice pointed out that petty corruption ('corruption on the streets') is measurable by the number of cases brought before the authorities, and this is very small. The culture in Finland is such that corrupt behaviours of this sort would be reported. On the other hand, grand corruption ('corruption in the suites') is much harder to identify as it is woven into the fabric of business, and less likely to come to the attention of the authorities (Joutsen & Keranen, 2009). In these sorts of activities there is often a mixing of legal and illegal, ethical and unethical behaviours, and much debate about where lines are drawn.

The real dilemma is whether the more acceptable approach is to change individuals' behaviour or the environment within which individuals live, work and play. Amitai Etzioni wrote perceptively over 40 years ago about how better results came from changing the environment rather than changing behaviour (Etzioni, 1977). He noted that advertising road safety and driver education in 1970 saved lives at a cost of $88,000 per life. Installing seat belts at $87 per belt saved as many lives. He points out that advertising temperance to alcoholics, world government to nationalist chauvinists, drug abstention to addicts and racial harmony to racists are not likely to achieve results. However, changing environments and putting in place protective or preventive factors may well do so. Does the same lesson apply to corruption? In the crime-prevention literature, making crime harder to commit is seen to be as valuable as trying to change the behaviour of offenders (Clarke, 2008; Ekblom, 1999; Felson, 2002). What has been termed 'situational prevention' is currently being applied to the study of corruption (Gorta, 1998; Graycar & Sidebottom, 2012), and will be explored further in later chapters.

Examples

In rich countries there are examples of politicians selling influence or being persuaded to do so. Here are some historical examples.

In 2009 the London press carried the allegation that four peers – Lord Truscott (former Energy Minister), Lord Moonie (former Defence Minister), Lord Snape and Lord Taylor – offered to help undercover reporters posing as lobbyists by using their influence to amend legislation in return for cash (http://www.guardian.co.uk/politics/2009/jan/25/lords-house-commons-corruption-allegations). Lord Truscott and Lord Taylor were recorded as saying that they helped clients in securing bills going through parliament. While Lord Truscott claimed he had helped to ensure that the Energy Bill was favourable to a client, Lord Taylor said that he had changed the law to help a credit check company. The lords were not prosecuted, since the evidence was too difficult to gather, and it was left to the House of Lords ethics committee to deal with them.

A celebrated case in Queensland, Australia, in 1970 involved a major aluminium company, Comalco, offering heavily discounted shares in the company to state ministers whose portfolios were relevant to the company (Wanna & Arklay, 2010, pp. 308–330). Ministers including the Treasurer (the Finance Minister), the Works and Housing Minister, the Conservation Minister, the Local Government Minister and the Industrial Development Minister all accepted the shares, as did some very senior bureaucrats. Had they sold when the shares were floated they would have made more money on the transaction than the average annual male wage.

10.1057/9781137335098

In order to prevent damaging fluctuations in milk production in the USA, the federal government instituted a policy of milk-price-support subsidies. In 1971 the President, Richard Nixon, raised the level of federal milk-price-support subsidies for dairy farmers. This provided a multi-million-dollar benefit to dairy farmers and raised the price of dairy products for US consumers. It was universally agreed that the level of the subsidy announced by President Nixon had no economic foundation, and it was greatly in excess of that recommended (and previously announced) by the Secretary of Agriculture. The intervention of the President came two days after he had met with dairy industry lobbyists at the White House who re-confirmed a very large ($2 million) contribution to President Nixon's re-election campaign (US Congress Senate, 1974).

In these three examples the common theme is that there is corruption in *making* public policy. In the House of Lords case, policy was for sale across a spectrum of government services, while in the others policy was being made about aluminium manufacture and milk pricing. What we see were monumental lapses of integrity rather than base criminality. The apparatus of government was used to distort policy outcomes in the milk case, and to lay the base for future favourable outcomes in the Comalco case.

These types of examples are different from cases where officials distort policies that are already in operation. We can document cases of an official in the tax department corruptly altering returns so that people who had bribed him would pay less tax; of politicians seeking bribes in order to facilitate the issuing of visas to immigrants; the issuing of licences or permits, for a personal fee, to people who are not qualified or do not meet the criteria; bribery in inspection of health and safety regulations; and on and on. These are cases of corruption in the implementation of public policy. Both of these types of cases – corrupting the making of policy and corrupting the implementation of policy – happen in rich countries.

One particularly egregious example occurred in Pennsylvania in the USA. In February 2009 two judges in the state of Pennsylvania, Judge Mark Ciavarella and Judge Michael T. Conahan, were indicted for having accepted $2.6 million in kickbacks over five years from the operators of two private prisons for juveniles. Basically they sentenced kids to prison terms in return for personal cash payments (Ecenbarger, 2012).

They had arranged the funding for two private detention centres to be built, they had the state-funded centre closed down, and then for a kickback ensured that the private centres had lots of clients. The judges would remand in custody of juveniles who had committed minor infractions, mostly against the recommendations of probation case officers. Seventeen-year-old Hilary Transue appeared before Judge Ciavarella for building a spoof webpage mocking one of her school teachers. She stated on the webpage that it was a joke, and despite never having been in any legal trouble before, she was led from the court in handcuffs to serve a three-month prison sentence on a charge of harassment.

Another youngster was jailed for trespassing, another for a minor shoplifting offence, another for giving a friend a black eye in a schoolyard altercation. Sometimes the kids would be in custody for many months before their cases were heard and then, more often than not, dismissed. The sentences that these two judges handed out were considerably outside the range of those given by other judges. The more juveniles sentenced to the private facility, the more money it made, and the more money the judges made.

In rich countries we expect that the administration of law and justice should be beyond corruption. In 2011 Conahan was sentenced to 17 years in prison, while Ciavarella received a sentence of 28 years.

How and why corruption arises

In all societies, and especially in rich countries, corruption certainly has an effect on public policy. It is important to distinguish between corruption in the *input* side of policy (the making of laws, policies, rules and regulations), and in the *output* side of policy (the implementation of laws and rules, the maintenance of health and safety regulations, the fair administration of justice and the equitable provision of public services).

A careful analysis of corruption in both the input and output sides of public policy points to a number of contextual attributes. In Chapter 1 it was noted that the unit of analysis in this book is the corrupt event. Examining some of the events described, one needs to make a judgement as to whether the context for corruption is *structural* or *opportunistic and episodic*. Is the corruption embedded in a total culture, pervading societies and organizations and tolerated either willingly or grudgingly? This is certainly the case in some of the syndromes described by Johnston (above). In some systems bribery is the grease behind every transaction, or delivery of every service.

10.1057/9781137335098

Or does a good opportunity to bribe or extort come out of a particular situation? Does a situation suddenly present itself – an opportunity arise unexpectedly, perhaps from employment in certain places which provides opportunities to exploit one's position? That would make the corruption situational. A police officer might catch somebody speeding and see an opportunity to take a bribe. Most of his or her colleagues would not do this. This is situational rather than structural. Virtually all judges in rich countries administer and dispense justice according to the law and ethically. But the judges above took opportunities that were situational rather than structural.

We should also ask whether those involved in the corrupt event were willing or unwilling participants. In a situation in which a police officer takes a bribe to look the other way and not give a ticket, there are two willing participants. In a case where the officer stops somebody who is not speeding and says that unless a bribe is paid he or she will write a ticket for speeding, the victim is unwilling. In the former case there has been *collusion*, in the latter extortion. Collusion involves willing partners seeking to obtain an unfair advantage for both. Extortion usually benefits only one person. The victim of extortion receives, after a payment, that which should have been theirs by right or law, or pays simply to receive fair treatment.

Are there opportunities for individuals to manufacture corrupt opportunities? What are the structural and value dynamics for this to occur? Are the perpetrators of a corrupt event acting alone, or in conjunction with others in their workplace?

To continue the analysis, is the corrupt event meant to benefit an individual or an organization? Not all corrupt events are for the benefit of individuals. When an individual is a beneficiary the motivation for the behaviour is sometimes need, to relieve poverty or deprivation, and sometimes it is pure greed. There are, of course, other motivations for corrupt behaviour. Somebody may wish to exhibit the patronage they can dispense, show that they can fix getting somebody a job, a good deal, a great benefit or a terrific opportunity. They can dispense this patronage to family or associates, and thus the behaviour is nepotistic or smacks of cronyism. There are also examples of corruption in exchange for love or friendship. A recent case involved a woman working in a passport office conducting improper transactions in visas for friends of her boyfriend. Her relationship was shaky, and by doing (illegal) favours she was hoping for gratitude and love in return (de Graaf & Huberts, 2008).

10.1057/9781137335098

Some corrupt events are undertaken to further causes. A teacher might be employed, not because they are the best teacher, but because they believe in certain political or religious values that a principal may want inculcated into pupils. An accountant might be hired knowing they could be relied upon to overlook the misallocation of resources to an organization that promotes specific causes or values.

What is it that is being corrupted? Perhaps it is a process, perhaps a culture, perhaps an event, or any combination of these. The corrupt judges corrupted a judicial process, they undermined a culture of fairness and impartiality, and in giving out custodial sentences for cash they corrupted events on specific days when the facility needed more customers. The peers who agreed to take money corrupted a culture of integrity, while a plumbing inspector would have corrupted a process. There are times when the corrupt behaviour demonstrates criminality, and cases of this sort find their way into the courts. At other times corruption comes from poor decision making or sloppy adherence to procedures.

Applying the variables laid out in this chapter and the previous one we can see that in the case of an inspector looking the other way the case might involve bribery, abuse of discretion, cronyism and acting alone. The opportunity was situational or opportunistic, an abuse of process and the actions were collusive. It was motivated by greed, and the loss to the city would have been a loss of governance capacity.

In the case of the politicians who accepted shares they were essentially trading in influence, and they demonstrated conflict of interest. The behaviour was structural in that it was embedded in the culture of the

TABLE 2.1   *A corruption checklist*

Corruption in	Are participants	Is the corruption
• The making of policy (input)	• Willing (collusion)	• Structural (embedded and/or tolerated)
• The implementation of policy (output)	• Unwilling (extortion)	• Opportunistic (episodic)
What is being corrupted?	Is the behaviour	Will the behaviour
• Process	• Criminal	• Benefit an individual or organization
• Culture	• Manipulative	• need/greed
• Event	• Poor process	• Exhibit patronage
	• Bad decision making	• nepotism / cronyism / love / friendship
		• Promote ideology, change values, re-allocate resources

time and tolerated. The participants were willing and there was collusion. It was hoped that their activities would favour an organization and greed dominated the situation.

In order to develop strategies to respond to any situation of corruption, readers may wish to apply the concepts above to specific cases of which they are aware.

It should be noted that in the same way that not all corruption is the same, responses to corruption are also not all the same. Different control mechanisms apply to controlling corruption in the input (making) and the output (implementing) sides of policy.

For example, in corruption in the making of policy, big-picture issues such as the strength of social capital, the degree of inequality in the society and adherence to the rule of law can shape the culture of corruption. There is also a place for sanctions and criminal penalties. On the other hand, controlling corruption in the implementation of policy might involve better processes in an organization, clear understandings of acceptable behaviour, although codes of conduct work best when there is supportive and ethical leadership committed to a clean culture. Whistleblowing has a place, as does the exploration of crime-prevention techniques. As a last resort criminal penalties have a place.

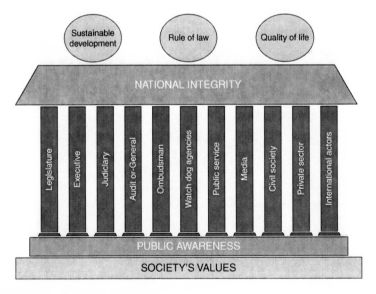

FIGURE 2.1 *The pillars of integrity*
Used with the permission of Transparancy International.

10.1057/9781137335098

Many of these will be discussed in chapters that follow, but most can be found in a study of the pillars of integrity that are present in any society.

The concept of a national integrity system was developed by Jeremy Pope at Transparency International (2000). It is depicted as a Greek temple, built on foundations of society's values and public awareness, and the individual pillars are a country's institutions, both public and private, such as the legislative and executive branches of government, the judiciary, the public sector, law enforcement, an electoral management body, the Ombudsman, an audit institution, anti-corruption agencies, political parties, media, civil society and business. These pillars in turn support the quality of life, the rule of law and sustainable development. In the business of international aid and development policies, an assessment of the strength of the pillars is a good indicator of integrity and transparency. In the analysis here, an assessment of the performance of the pillars, both individually and as a whole, helps us understand the integrity health of a system. When all the pillars in a National Integrity System are functioning well, corruption remains in check. If some or all of the pillars wobble, these weaknesses can allow corruption to thrive and damage a society (Transparency International, 2013).

10.1057/9781137335098

3
Measuring Corruption

Abstract: *Measuring corruption is difficult, and this chapter begins by explaining how the secretive and consensual nature of corruption tends to put it outside conventional crime statistics. Nonetheless, attempting to measure corruption is important, not least for the design and evaluation of anti-corruption measures. The chapter sets out a wide range of useful indicators, including public experience and perception surveys, employee and supplier surveys, focus groups and media reports, complaints and allegations, and prosecutions and convictions. Another approach involves risk-based analyses of institutions and sectors to assess their vulnerability to corruption. Each of these methods has particular advantages and limitations, but the greater the array of indicators employed the clearer the picture of corruption dimensions and trends.*

Graycar, Adam and Prenzler, Tim. *Understanding and Preventing Corruption.* Basingstoke: Palgrave Macmillan, 2013. DOI: 10.1057/9781137335098.

Measuring what?

This book opened with the assertion that there is probably no more corruption today than there has been in the past. This was an assertion because measuring corruption is a hugely difficult task. We know it when we see it, or at least we think we do. But we do not define it precisely, and so if it is not defined, how can we measure it? And if we measure what we think it is, what are we trying to communicate, and how prone to error are we? If we were to measure corruption, how would we use that measure, and who would be interested?

It is important to measure corruption for two main reasons. First, it is an indicator of how well a society is performing in terms of a government's contract with its citizens. If there is bribery, extortion, misappropriation, self-dealing, if major capital and development projects serve an individual's financial interests rather than the public interest, if foreign corporations bribe public officials to exploit natural resources, if human rights abuses are tolerated, if justice administration is inconsistent with the rule of law, then that society is more corrupt than those in which these behaviours are less or not part of the social fabric. Measuring these characteristics, either singly or in some aggregated form, gives an understanding of the potential for that country to be a significant player in global governance or international business, and whether investing in that country would be sound. Overall these measures can focus attention on the existence of corruption and start to shape actions to temper it.

Second, if we know how much corruption there is within a country and the nature and quantity of those corrupt events, then remedial actions can be put in place and preventive measures can be implemented. This is a means of establishing confidence in institutions and a sense of pride and security within the citizenry that their lives and behaviours are governed by rules appropriately arrived at and administered fairly. Furthermore if interventions have been put in place, measuring corruption gives an indication of how successful these measures may have been – it can evaluate progress in anti-corruption and identify what sorts of things work best.

However, most of the traditional measurement methods of the social sciences do not apply. There is very little administrative data on corruption. We have reliable data on numbers of burglaries, car thefts and homicides, for example, since there are reports to police, claims on insurance,

10.1057/9781137335098

bodies found and so on. For crimes such as rape or assault the statistics are less reliable, since not all are reported, but there are surveys of victims and these can be compared with reports to police. With corruption the activity is nearly always covert. If there is collusion, then it is in neither party's interest to report it and have the activity counted in any way. If the behaviour were extortion, it would be rare for a complaint to be made to the authorities, and if it were, the charge that might be brought could be something like obtaining money with menaces, some form of theft, or breach of a public service provision. As corrupt behaviour is usually dealt with under the heading of a different offence, even identifying what instances of a criminal act could be called corrupt can be very difficult.

Because of its clandestine nature many of the measures of corruption that we see are not therefore measures of corrupt *behaviour*, but instead measures of people's *perception* of corruption – perceptions of its incidence and perceptions of its nature. They are, in effect, proxy measurements. These measurements, it should be noted, are usually not measures of the damage caused by corruption.

As Angela Gorta points out, measuring corruption is not an end in its own right. Corruption measurement is simply a tool to achieve a purpose. When considering the question of how to measure corruption, one should first consider why one is seeking to do so (Gorta, 2006). As this chapter unfolds, we will explore reasons for measuring and techniques of measurement, and describe some of the measures that are used around the world.

Heinrich and Hodess (2011) have written of how the measurement of corruption has evolved (see Table 3.1). They trace three generations of corruption measurement tools whose objectives, over time, were:

1   putting corruption on the map;
2   benchmarking across time and space;
3   assessing specific corruption risks.

The *first-generation* tools sought to rank countries and set up perceptions. These were awareness-raising activities that in some cases guided policy makers, investors and donors. Notable here are the Transparency International Corruption Perception Index (CPI) and the World Bank's Governance Indicators (WBGI). They have established important benchmarks and heightened awareness of the issues, and have become more refined over time.

The *second-generation* tools sought to benchmark progress over time and to examine experiences of people exposed to corruption, and also

TABLE 3.1   *Key features of measurement tool generations*

	Composite indicators (1st generation)	Comparative meso-level assessments (2nd generation)	Country-specific multi-method assessments (3rd generation)
Primary purpose	Awareness-raising, naming & shaming	Benchmarking across time & space	Diagnosis, recommendation & policy/advocacy
Main output	Single ranking	Multiple rankings; comparative reports	In-depth corruption or governance assessment
Level of aggregation	High	Medium	Low
Data	Expert perceptions	Expert assessments or experiential surveys	Multiple data sources; focus on triangulation
Primary unit of analysis	Country	Governance system	Institution, sector, policy, subsystem
Main target group	Senior government, international business leaders, media	International donors, business sectors	Donors in-country, local civil society, public officials
Ownership	International institution	International institution, in co-operation with country partners	Country stakeholders, with technical support from international institution

Source: Heinrich and Hodess (2011 p. 29). Used with the permission of Edward Elgar.

to measure how systems set processes to minimize corruption. To measure impacts there are global crime victimization surveys such as the International Crime Victim Survey and Transparency International's Global Corruption Barometer (see Table 3.2). These two are surveys that measure a mixture of behaviour and perceptions. The second set of second-generation tools also includes measures of the integrity pillars (see Chapter 2). They assess the strength and performance of institutions and anti-corruption systems in various countries. The Global Integrity Index and the Open Budget Index are examples of this sort of activity. The World Bank has developed a Public Expenditure and Financial Accountability Framework (PEFA) as a proxy corruption measure.

The *third-generation* tools focus on assessing specific corruption risks and, as their tools of analysis, examine institutions, laws and policies, sub-systems and processes and sectors. This enables measurement along the lines of the TASP approach outlined in Chapter 1, where components are identified, broken down and then re-aggregated to give a bigger

10.1057/9781137335098

picture. Examples here come out of measures used to evaluate the United Nations Convention against Corruption and the OECD Anti-Bribery Convention, as well as studies of specific institutions such as courts or legislatures or sectors such as mining, health or transport.

While this covers the broad sweep of measuring big-picture corruption, focusing on activities and events can be more difficult. Methodological skill is required to measure the occurrence, the types and the costs and effects of corruption. One study conducted by one of the authors used a methodology that took 100 consecutive cases in which the New York City Department of Investigation (DOI) had arrested a person for corruption.

The 100 cases were what happened to be on the books during a specific period of time. They signified not the full quantum of corruption in New York City during that period, but the corruption cases that came within the jurisdiction of the agency, the DOI. The DOI did not have jurisdiction over police corruption, for example. It was not possible from this study to measure the incidence or prevalence of corruption in NYC, let alone in the USA. It was not possible to determine motives for corruption by the perpetrators. What the study was able to do was identify the types of corruption, make some assessment of the costs and effects, and start to identify some preventive counter-measures (Graycar & Villa, 2011). As noted in Chapter 2 most events involved a low-level officer, working alone and taking bribes of small monetary value. The loss to the city was primarily a loss of governance capacity.

Measuring Corruption Risk

Gorta writes that identifying high-risk functions, and then assessing whether these are part of an organization's activity, allows us to understand where an organization may fit into a corruption-risk assessment. She lists a number of high-risk functions:

1　inspecting, regulating or monitoring standards of premises, businesses, equipment or products;
2　providing a service to new immigrants;
3　issuing qualifications or licences to individuals to indicate their proficiency or enable them to undertake certain types of activities;
4　providing a service to the community where demand frequently exceeds supply;
5　allocating grants of public funds;
6　issuing, or reviewing the issue of, fines or other sanctions;

7   receiving cash payments;

8   providing assistance or care to the vulnerable or disabled;

9   providing subsidies, financial assistance, concessions or other relief to those in need;

10   making determinations/handing down judgments about individuals or disputes;

11   testing blood, urine or other bodily samples from people or animals;

12   having discretion concerning land rezoning or development applications;

13   selling tickets;

14   undertaking construction; and

15   having regular dealings with the private sector other than for the routine purchasing of goods and services. (Gorta, 2006, p. 209)

Of course not all agencies do all or even most of these things, but understanding these can help develop measures of risk, opportunity and performance, and put risk-mitigation practices in place.

Measuring the extent of corruption

When we set out to measure corruption it's important always to ask: what is it that we want to know when we've made this measurement? Do we want to know how many corrupt acts have taken place? Or are we interested in knowing what organizational weaknesses lead to corrupt acts? Or is there something else again that we want to know? It would be naïve to expect the end result will be a single number or percentage.

Another project undertaken by one of the current authors involves assessing the extent of, opportunity for, and possible responses to corruption in the state of Victoria, Australia. By population, Victoria is the second largest state in Australia and its government covers the full range of governmental functions with all the associated corruption risks. A number of measures were used:

▸ a general poll of perceptions of corruption and confidence in institutions;

▸ a set of focus groups conducted with a cross-section of the community;

▸ a meticulous analysis of media reports of corruption;

10.1057/9781137335098

- a survey of senior civil servants;
- a survey of suppliers to the government;
- a desk analysis of the performance of integrity agencies;
- a desk review of integrity agencies outside Victoria for comparative and benchmarking purposes; and
- a survey of departmental heads to identify integrity practices in their agencies.

This mixture of methods does not give a composite measure of corruption, but it broadens understanding and allows for policy interventions based on judgements on the basis of the evidence.

The general poll mentioned above was a national survey, part of a regular Australian National University (ANU) series (McAllister et al., 2012). Polls of this nature are not cheap; they can cost around $100,000 to conduct. This poll covered perceptions of corruption, and it added these to long-standing questions (that had been asked in previous polls) about confidence in national institutions and views of problems affecting the country. It oversampled for the state of Victoria so that the responses were sufficient for statistical analysis.

The findings showed that 43 per cent of the population thought that corruption had increased in Australia in the previous three years, and 7 per cent thought it had declined; yet fewer than one per cent of the population had experienced, in the previous five years, an official seeking a bribe from them (McAllister et al., 2012). When asked which institutions they thought were corrupt, the highest numbers named the media, political parties and trade unions (in that order). The institutions that the least numbers of people thought corrupt were the armed forces (least corrupt), the public service and the police.

The focus groups yielded similar results: many people expressed concerns that corruption was widespread, but very few were able to give examples of corrupt events that affected them, although there was some animosity towards politicians. However, the focus groups allowed for in-depth discussion of perceptions and institutions deemed to have potential for corruption.

The review of media reports found 5,000 references to corruption in the print media over the previous two years . However, only 16 per cent covered corruption in the state. Other reports were on international events and events in other parts of Australia, and the largest number of references was to corruption in films, fiction, historical literature and to activities that could only be marginally related to corruption. The results were classified according to the TASP framework in Chapter 1.

The survey of senior civil servants asked about their observations and suspicions of corruption in their departments and across other departments. It also asked whether respondents thought, when corruption was observed, that the response had been handled appropriately. The data from this survey are being analysed using the TASP framework, and will later be published. The survey of suppliers is currently being developed and will focus on actual experiences and responses, while the integrity survey will focus on practices that are in place, and opportunities for improvement.

The purpose of using this illustration is to show that there is no single measure that can be used. Any measurement involves many component parts, using different methodologies and negotiating different types of access to information. Negotiating access is a huge task, with many agencies nervous about participating, and this is in a country that is not noted for extensive corrupt practice in government administration. In general, senior officials and department heads were keen for the research to take place, while those at lower levels were lukewarm. Nor is it a cheap exercise. The surveys are costly to conduct and to analyse, as are the resources to gather information in desk reviews. However, small-scale measures can be conducted by academics working with groups of students, as a class exercise to both gather information and teach methodological skills.

Trying to measure corruption in one rich country, the Netherlands, gives further examples of the challenges involved. Huberts and his colleagues (Huberts et al., 2006) argue that there is more corruption than is reported or detected. As is the case in Australia, bribery is rare, but examples of unethical behaviour are not. The research team measured things like conflict of interest, improper use of authority, manipulation and misuse of information, discrimination and sexual harassment.

The researchers devised a triangle with a very broad base leading up to a narrow apex. From the bottom of the triangle the data sources, which became less plentiful as they went up to the apex, were (in order) self reports of deviant behaviour, self reports of victimization, corrupt behaviour in work environments as seen by colleagues, internal investigations, criminal cases and convictions. At the top of the pyramid they noted that there are very few convictions – fewer than 20 per year in the Netherlands, arising from between 20 and 50 court cases per year. The numbers are small, and show that legal mechanisms are often a very last resort.

10.1057/9781137335098

FIGURE 3.1   *Measuring corruption*
Source: Huberts et al., 2006. Used with the permission of Ashgate.

Corrupt behaviour in the work environment is a different story. The same research team studied 755 Dutch police officers and found 4 per cent observing bribery, 19 per cent observing favouritism towards family and friends, and 59 per cent perceiving undue favouritism by management. When a similar survey was conducted with 1,000 randomly selected workers in the Dutch labour force, the responses were similar, though somewhat higher: 7 per cent for bribery, 33 per cent favouritism towards family and friends, and 73 per cent favouritism by management. The Netherlands appears to be non-corrupt to most observers. It is only when one digs and looks for specific patterns in specific places that one gets some sorts of numbers upon which to base a discussion (Huberts et al., 2006).

But what is the real number? How do we arrive at a real number from a data source? In Australia's largest state, New South Wales, the Independent Commission against Corruption (ICAC) is kept very busy with complaints. NSW is perceived to be the most politically corrupt state in Australia and scandals are often in the media. But how much corruption is there? Do we examine only that which was reported to ICAC? In 2011–12 ICAC received 2,978 complaints; 2,255 led to no further action by ICAC, although about 200 of these were referred by ICAC to other agencies and 376 cases were referred to the Assessments Section for further enquiry (ICAC NSW, 2012a). In 73 of these cases investigations were commenced, and 54 were terminated after preliminary investigations were completed. Nineteen were escalated to full investigation. Of these ICAC will find some in breach of the rules, and will recommend remedial action or future prevention strategies, will find no wrongdoing in some and will refer some to the Director of Public Prosecution. For some of these a decision will be taken not to prosecute, and of those that are prosecuted not all will result in a conviction.

So with 2,978 complaints, of which 450 warranted some action and 19 are going to a full investigation, what is the number/rate/incidence/prevalence of corruption in the state? This pattern has prevailed in recent years. These data are reported openly and publicly, and the ICAC has a reputation for transparency in its operations and reports.

These examples of variability and methodological complexity in measurement have all related to rich countries. In poorer countries the task is much more difficult since data are rarely kept, and what data exist are rarely made available. The quality of the data may be questionable, and many regimes have no great reputation for transparency.

When dealing in the development arena, measurement tends to focus on the needs of the people (and how corruption has affected their well-being) and on the risk assessment of donor funds being diverted from their stated purpose. How do we measure the risk and effect of aid money not reaching its target?

Francesca Recanatini (2011) outlines a methodology for assessing different forms of corruption in a country, measuring social and economic costs of poor governance, and analysing a country's institutional structure and benchmarking various forms of public sector performance and extent of corruption. In addition to the institutional analysis she outlines how one might conduct a survey of public officials, a business survey and a household survey. This is based on the World Bank toolkit developed by the USAID Agency (2009).

This very detailed assessment is like a huge recipe book. It outlines step by step how to gather data about institutions and sectors and what sorts of questions to gather data on. Firstly it takes syndromes such as those proposed by Johnston (2005) (see page 24) and points out that different data need to be gathered for different syndromes. It lays out a detailed corruption-assessment framework, and shows how it can be applied. It provides templates for questionnaires that explore corruption in institutions, who the beneficiaries might be, how they do it, who wins and who loses. There are questions also about the institutional framework, the structure of services, conflict of interest, and administrative patterns and procurement. These are applied then to sectors, such as health, judiciary, education or customs.

In education, as in other sectors, there are dozens of questions, including the following:

- Does the teaching staff often sell examination questions, marks, report cards/certificates?
- Do teachers often change grades for fees?
- Are students forced to buy certain materials or additional materials?
- Are they forced to take private lessons or to provide special payments or services?
- Are teachers' salaries unreasonably low?
- Are teachers paid on time?
- Are teachers often absent because of other income-producing work?
- Do budget funds reach the intended school or are they often diverted?
- Are administrative procedures easy to understand and transparent?
- Are budgets and financial transactions easily manipulated?
- Does the administration have adequate reporting and documentation?
- Do schools collect funds from parents for school needs in a transparent manner, i.e., providing parents with information on needs and expenditures? Do parents participate in managing extra-budgetary funds?
- Are unauthorized fees imposed on students?
- Do inspectors typically overlook school violations for a fee/favour?
- Do school supplies reach their intended destination or are they diverted?

Questions such as these are structured under diagnostic headings such as sector overview, budget clarity, accountability, transparency,

10.1057/9781137335098

complaints mechanisms, financial control and oversight, integrity mechanisms and so on.

These are not easy questions on which to obtain data, but the many toolkits developed by agencies like Transparency International, USAID and other national aid agencies, World Bank, Asian Development Bank provide very good guidance for people collecting data. Search the internet for 'measuring corruption' and a host of sources and toolkits will be available to you.

Measuring the costs of corruption

There are different ways of assessing the costs of corruption. Oxford Policy Management (2007) lists at least four:

1   Estimates of grand corruption by political leaders;
2   Surveys of households and firms on bribe payments;
3   Public expenditure tracking surveys;
4   Econometrically modelled estimates that encompass both direct and indirect costs.

While these measures identify many billions of dollars looted by leaders such as Suharto, Marcos, Mobutu and Fujimori, this can only be an indicator, since more information needs to be gathered on how the funds were looted and how widespread was the looting. It does, however, send a signal to investors and potential donors. Household and business surveys yield good results, although they are costly, and respondents sometimes have apprehensions about participating in surveys of this sort. The World Bank has developed a substantial methodology for the tracking of public sector expenditure and the effects of programmes poorly delivered, as well as a host of econometric techniques.

A novel approach was developed by Harvard economist Benjamin Olken (2007), who was studying corruption in road-building in Indonesia. He measured the number of dollars in aid, the amount of cement and other materials needed to build a road, and then did an analysis of a few chunks of road – they were dug up, and a forensic engineering examination calculated how much material was actually used. It was a lot less than funded: the difference had been skimmed off. Olken's work was not aimed at measuring the road properties, but rather different types of monitoring for corruption. The result showed that

10.1057/9781137335098

monitoring by government officials was more likely to reduce corruption than monitoring locally. This is an example of one type of measurement that has policy implications.

Other measures

Transparency International has developed what is perhaps the most widely known and used data index, the *Corruption Perception Index* (CPI). This has been issued each year since 1995. It scores countries on how corrupt their public sectors are perceived to be. There are 176 countries listed in the index. The top countries (perceived to be least corrupt in 2012) are Denmark, Finland, New Zealand (sharing the top rank), Sweden and Singapore, Australia and Norway. Those perceived to be at the bottom in 2012 are Afghanistan, North Korea, Somalia (sharing the bottom rank), Sudan , Myanmar, Uzbekistan and Iraq.

The Index was developed by German academic Johann Graf Lambsdorff and it draws on assessments from a dozen different studies conducted by organizations such as the World Bank, Africa Development Bank, Asian Development Bank, Bertelsmann (Transformation Index), World Economic Forum and Economist Intelligence Unit. To be included in the CPI, a source must measure the overall extent of corruption (frequency and/or size of corrupt transactions) in the public and political sectors and provide a ranking of countries. A country must be covered by a minimum of three of the sources of information TI uses for the CPI to be ranked in the Index.

There are two different types of sources. The first one is businesspeople opinion surveys. The second one is assessments (scores) of a country's performance as provided by a group of country/risk/expert analysts. Opinion surveys, where possible, are averaged over a two-year period. Not all sources rank all countries in the index. A methodological paper (Transparency International, 2010) describes the scaling system, the confidence intervals and the ranking method in some detail.

As noted above, corruption is a clandestine activity, and the CPI uses proxy measures (in this case, third-party perceptions) and then aggregates them and subjects them to rigorous statistical refinement. The commentators are mostly businesspeople or country specialists, not the citizens in the countries nor the victims of corruption. This has led to considerable criticism of the Index.

10.1057/9781137335098

TABLE 3.2   *Some corruption measures*

Corruption Perception Index (Transparency International)	http://www.transparency.org/research/cpi/overview
Bribe Payers Index (Transparency International)	http://bpi.transparency.org/bpi2011/
Governance and Corruption Diagnostic Survey (World Bank)	http://web.worldbank.org/WBSITE/EXTERNAL/WBI/EXTWBIGOVANTCOR/0,,contentMDK:20726148~pagePK:64168445~piPK:64168309~theSitePK:1740530,00.html
Worldwide Governance Indicators (World Bank)	http://info.worldbank.org/governance/wgi/index.aspx#home
Global Corruption Barometer (Transparency International)	http://www.transparency.org/research/gcb/overview
International Crime Victims Survey	http://www.unicri.it/services/library_documentation/publications/icvs/

However, there is no denying that countries perceived as the least corrupt, rich countries in northern Europe (and New Zealand and Singapore), are in a different league when compared to the embattled poor, desperate and sometimes war-torn countries in Africa and central and south Asia where poverty and corruption are rife. Issues of dispute usually arise in respect of countries that lie in the middle of the long table. Countries sometimes significantly improve or diminish their standing and this is a cause for domestic political comment.

The 2011 *Bribe Payers Index* (also produced by Transparency International) ranks the likelihood of companies from 28 leading economies to win business abroad by paying bribes. The Index first appeared in 1999, and until 2008 it comprised 22 mostly rich countries. In 2011 Argentina, Indonesia, Malaysia, Saudi Arabia, Turkey and the United Arab Emirates were added to the Index. The methodology is described at http://bpi.transparency.org/bpi2011/in_detail/ and consists of asking about 3,000 senior business executives from 30 countries for their perceptions of the likelihood of companies, from countries they have business dealings with, to engage in bribery when doing business in the executive's country. A country's Bribe Payers Index score is an average of the scores given by all the respondents who rated that country. Although the BPI focuses on bribery by the corporate sector, and the CPI focuses on perceptions of public sector corruption, there is a strong correlation between standings on both scales.

The countries in which businesses are perceived to be the least likely to pay bribes are the Netherlands, Switzerland, Belgium, Germany,

Japan, Australia and Canada and those perceived to be the most likely are Russia, China, Mexico, Indonesia, the United Arab Emirates, and Argentina. The study ranks 19 sectors for perceptions of bribery; those least likely to have bribery as common features are agriculture, light manufacturing, civilian aerospace and information technology. The sectors most susceptible to bribery are perceived to be public works and construction, utilities, real estate and property, oil and gas, and mining.

The *Global Corruption Barometer* is a global public opinion survey on corruption. In 2010 and 2011 the Barometer interviewed more than 100,000 people in 100 countries. The Barometer explores the general public's views about corruption levels in their country as well as their governments' efforts to fight corruption. The 2010/11 Barometer also probes the frequency of bribery, reasons for paying a bribe during the preceding year and attitudes towards reporting incidents of corruption. The methodology and the data can be downloaded from http://gcb. transparency.org/gcb201011/in_detail/.

The dataset is huge and shows that an average of 58 per cent of people believe that corruption has increased in their country during the preceding 12 months. In most countries a majority believes it has increased. Yet when asked whether they had personally paid a bribe, the numbers were considerably lower. Twenty-four per cent of people reported having paid a bribe, ranging from zero in Denmark to 87 per cent in Uganda and 89 per cent in Liberia. The data from Denmark mirror those found in Australia reported above (page 39). In Denmark, nobody reported having paid a bribe, yet 29 per cent believe corruption is on the increase.

Another question asked whether people believed the government was effective in fighting corruption. According to the results, 31 per cent believed it was effective, with 50 per cent believing it was ineffective. The countries where government was thought to be most effective were Fiji, Georgia and Cambodia – countries that do not have good track records in anti-corruption or human rights! The least effective were perceived to be Yemen, Spain, Portugal, Israel and Ireland. Again in Denmark, the top country on TI's CPI, 44 per cent thought the government was ineffective in fighting corruption. It is gratifying to see that the overwhelming majority of people in most countries stated they would report an incident of corruption, including 92 per cent in Denmark.

The World Bank has attempted to quantify the quality of governance, and has developed the *Worldwide Governance Indicators* (WGI) project, which reports aggregate and individual governance indicators for 215 economies over the period 1996–2011, for six dimensions of governance:

1 Voice and accountability;
2 Political stability and absence of violence;
3 Government effectiveness;
4 Regulatory quality;
5 Rule of law; and
6 Control of corruption.

The World Bank has also undertaken a number of Country Diagnostic Surveys, and data on about 20 countries can be found on this website. Surveys complement the macro-level Worldwide Governance Indicators in that they operate at the micro- or sub-national level and use information gathered from a country's own citizens, businesspeople and public sector workers to diagnose governance vulnerabilities and suggest concrete approaches for fighting corruption. The use of rigorous statistical methods generates a quantifiable baseline which can be used to set targets and hold leadership accountable for reform progress.

Before the CPI became a standard measure of corruption in 1995, analyses were mostly qualitative, episodic and limited. There have been many critiques of the methodology of the CPI (for example, Andersson & Heywood, 2009), while Hansen (2012) doubts that 'such a highly controversial, hyper complex, concealed and basically immeasurable phenomenon' can be measured at all, let alone reduced to a single number. When the CPI was developed, wrote Ivan Krastev:

> the impact of the corruption index was shattering. All major newspapers around the world published it and commented on it. Opposition parties started to refer to it. Governments began attacking it. However, the most important effect was the public conviction that it was possible to compare levels in certain countries and to monitor the rise of corruption in any one individual country. (Krastev, quoted in Hansen, 2012, p. 515)

Performance indexes are rarely anchored in or supported by traditional regulatory frameworks, writes Hansen (2012, p. 508), yet they extend into the transnational realm and connect individual and organizational to globalizing ideals about what is good and bad behaviour. Numbers are not just performance measures, but are important mechanisms to foster social identities, to define group characteristics and structure behaviour so that reality and expectations can come closer.

10.1057/9781137335098

Part II
Designing Counter-Measures

10.1057/9781137335098

4

The Architecture of Corruption Control

Abstract: *This first chapter in Part II of the book on designing counter-measures sets out the basic legal and institutional framework required to explicitly address and minimize corruption. Complex measures are required to address the complex nature of corruption. The importance of comprehensive and clear legal prohibitions on corrupt behaviour is highlighted. Emphasis is also placed on the need to follow through from rule setting to adequate deterrence and control through investigations and prosecutions. In a growing number of jurisdictions this is achieved through specialist anti-corruption agencies. International treaties are also described which support efforts within and between countries to eliminate, or at least limit, corruption, including through the dissemination of regular corruption risk assessments and reports.*

Graycar, Adam and Prenzler, Tim. *Understanding and Preventing Corruption*. Basingstoke: Palgrave Macmillan, 2013. DOI: 10.1057/9781137335098.

10.1057/9781137335098

Like everything that has to do with corruption, the control of corruption is a multi-faceted activity. In order to work on it one must know what it is, but definitions are contentious. One should be able to measure how much there is, and measures are controversial. Luis de Sousa makes the point that in anti-corruption activity there are no individual solutions but a cocktail of measures (de Sousa, 2010, p. 19).

Most obviously and commonly, governments pass legislation that makes it an offence to engage in corrupt behaviour. However, one cannot make a law to cover every type of corrupt behaviour. Most frequently, we see legislation to outlaw bribery, and indeed, most countries have statutes that prohibit bribery. However, the scope of these laws varies. Some include bribery of foreign officials; others do not. Many include bribery in the private sector; others do not. In many countries, elected officials (and in particular members of parliament) are not held to the same strict standards in respect of bribery as are public officials. As for other forms of corruption, a number of countries define trading in influence, illicit enrichment or nepotism as a separate offence; many others do not. Many countries have a catch-all offence commonly known as abuse of public office, which can be used to deal with corruption. The scope of this offence, however, varies considerably. Embezzlement and misappropriation by a public official are almost universally criminalized.

The UK has recently overhauled its legislation by adopting the Bribery Act 2010. It specifies the crimes of bribery, being bribed, the bribery of foreign public officials and the failure of a commercial organization to prevent bribery on its behalf. The Bribery Act imposes high standards and prescribes severe penalties. In Australia, various sections of the Commonwealth Criminal Code prohibit bribery of a public official and of a foreign official, as well as trading in influence or abusing public office. Embezzlement or misappropriation by a public official are covered by the Financial Management and Accountability Act, 1997. In other countries similar bits and pieces make up the legislative landscape. Legislation, however, is of limited value unless there is capacity and willingness for enforcement. As with crime prevention, the prevention of corruption does not work effectively if criminalization and the threat of punishment are the only tools. Often organizational capacity building and anti-corruption agencies are the conduit for more effective prevention and enforcement.

Many countries have set up anti-corruption agencies (ACAs); some have been successful and some glaringly less so. While Singapore,

Malaysia and Hong Kong established ACAs in 1952, 1967 and 1974 respectively, and New York City as long ago as 1873, most ACAs that currently exist came into operation in the 1990s or 2000s (Heilbrunn, 2004).

Anti-corruption agencies

An ACA is a public agency whose task is to fight corruption, reduce opportunities for corruption, develop preventive mechanisms and create public awareness of the ill effects of corruption. A typical ACA also has the authority to investigate corrupt events and refer corrupt perpetrators for legal sanction or punishment (but not to administer the punishment themselves). However, not all ACAs have this investigative function. ACAs are established for the long term, in contrast to a commission of inquiry or short-term investigation.

For a hundred years under colonial rule, Hong Kong developed into a monumentally corrupt society where police and low-level officials took bribes and extorted money and other benefits across a number of fronts (ICAC Hong Kong, 2011). Police took 'tea money' (unlawful payments) to do their job, and this became syndicated so that everybody got a share. The cop on the street would give some to his superior, and so on up the chain. This story was repeated in several government departments. In 1975 Peter Godber, a very senior police officer who had fled from Hong Kong to the UK to avoid prosecution for corruption, was extradited, tried and imprisoned. Before his case was finalized the Hong Kong Legislative Council created an Independent Commission against Corruption (ICAC) and in the decades since its establishment it has been held up as a shining and successful example of corruption control.

This ACA was established as a response to a crisis situation, one that the community would not tolerate. A similar story can be told of the Crime and Misconduct Commission (CMC) in Queensland, Australia (Prenzler, 2011). Following an extensive inquiry in 1990 (by a Royal Commission) which found that corruption was endemic within the government of Queensland as well as within the police, the CMC was established, again in response to a crisis situation.

As noted, New York City established an ACA in 1873. Over the years, New York City officials (like many city officials elsewhere) had gained notoriety for perpetrating corruption, fraud, bribery and theft with impunity. However, it was not possible for the New York Police Department

(NYPD) to tackle all these cases effectively without jeopardizing their major role of maintaining law and order in the city and protecting the people from violent crime.

The Department of Investigation (DOI) was founded in 1873 to serve as an independent and non-partisan watchdog for the New York City government, and was specifically delegated the role of dealing promptly and effectively with cases of corruption which were eating into the coffers of the city government. Its main role is to combat corruption in public institutions in New York City and ensure that public officials do not use their position for private gain. See http://www.nyc.gov/html/doi/html/about/history.shtml for the history of the DOI.

The DOI consists of attorneys, investigators, forensic auditors, computer forensic specialists and administrative personnel, and its major functions include investigating and referring for criminal prosecution cases of fraud, corruption and unethical conduct by city employees, contractors and others who receive city money. There are 300,000 employees of the New York City government, so the task is huge. The DOI also studies agency procedures to identify corruption hazards and recommends improvements in order to reduce the city's vulnerability to fraud, waste and corruption. It recovers the city's stolen funds and protects the city's finances by pursuing criminal and civil forfeiture, restitution and other types of financial recovery. Because of DOI investigations, 'in 2009 more than $27 million was ordered or agreed to in restitution, fines, forfeitures and other financial recoveries on behalf of the City and other victims' (Gill Hearn, 2009, p. 4).

ACAs exist in many other jurisdictions. In Singapore the Corruption Prevention Investigation Bureau (CPIB) was established in 1952 following an instance of police stealing drugs and belonging to a drug distribution syndicate. In New South Wales, Australia, an ICAC was established in 1988, not in response to a specific crisis, but because corruption was seen to be widespread and in need of control. Other Australian states have established similar ACAs with varying resources and mandates, and have done so as a part of routine government policy rather than in response to a crisis.

Singapore academic John Quah has studied Asian ACAs in great detail, comparing and contrasting them, and evaluated their success (2003). Singapore and Hong Kong, despite significant budget differences between the two agencies, are the examples of success that he cites. The one factor in common, above all others, that Quah attributes their effectiveness to, is political will. Where there is political will to support anti-corruption, where governments provide resources and implement the rule of law, then the ACA will be more successful. Quah deems the (Indian) Central Bureau of Investigation (CBI) not to be a success. He analyses performance and budgets, and uses two data sources, the continually slipping ranking of India on Transparency International's Corruption Perception Index and the number of Indians reporting that they pay bribes, to support his judgement (2003, ch. 3).

In another study Quah (2010) compares ACAs in Singapore, Hong Kong, South Korea and Thailand, and introduces another data variable, ease of doing business. Singapore and Hong Kong are much higher on the CPI ranking, and also much easier places in which to do business. Again, he attributes the differences and the better performance in anti-corruption to political will.

So what is it that makes an ACA perform well? For example the Hong Kong ICAC is characterized by the following:

▶ a single organization with a de facto monopoly over corruption control rather than multiple anti-corruption organizations performing the same function;
▶ independence from government;
▶ a strategy of prevention, education and sanction that is reflected organizationally in the division of the ICAC into Corruption Prevention, Community Relations and Operations Departments;
▶ extensive powers that include the right of arrest and detention;
▶ secure funding even in the face of major cutbacks in public expenditure;
▶ personnel of the highest moral calibre;
▶ the political will to combat corruption; and
▶ public support of sufficient strength to the extent that the ICAC has repeatedly been found to be the most trusted organization in Hong Kong. (Scott, 2011b)

The things that stand out from many observations is that a mixture of political will, strong and enforceable laws, and a coherent strategy of investigation, prevention and education are pointers to success. These need to be complemented by good management practices and good co-operation between managers and prevention people in agencies, and investigation officers who know what sort of corruption is predominant at any time.

10.1057/9781137335098

There are now hundreds of ACAs around the world. A full list (and all of their websites) can be found on the United Nations Office of Drugs and Crime's excellent TRACK site http://www.track.unodc.org/ACAuthorities/Pages/home.aspx.

De Sousa's article (2010), 'Anti-corruption Agencies: Between Empowerment and Irrelevance', sums up the wide spectrum across which ACAs work. He says that some have seen their capabilities grow over time (for example, Lithuania, Romania), some have been abolished (Italy, Portugal, South Africa), while others are minnows and largely unknown (such as Malta and Mozambique) (p. 19). It is always difficult to predict how effective an ACA might be, and whether its success, rather than its failure, might be its path to abolition. Michela Wrong (2009) writes about the ACA in Kenya which was eliminated when the director started to investigate the activities of those in top political positions. When the NSW ICAC was established in 1988, its first focus of inquiry was the premier (head of state government) who had set it up. He resigned (and was later fully exonerated). In this case, the subsequent power and impact of the ICAC was not diminished because it targeted a political leader.

Common to successful ACAs are a number of characteristics, outlined by de Sousa (2010, pp. 13–18). As noted above, they must be independent: exempt from political interference and trusted freely to pursue their policy objectives. Part of this independence is that they recruit on merit and have budgetary autonomy. Consolidating that independence is a challenge of political will, especially given that their budgets are set by legislatures. It is important also that they are free to discuss their work (as appropriate) in the media.

There must be inter-institutional co-operation and networking. International ACAs work across borders, since corruption is not confined to national boundaries. National ACAs should be completely separate from other government agencies, but have full co-operation from these agencies when doing their work. Their work is specialized, and this requires specialized staff. They need to be people of great intellect, flexible and well trained. Independence of recruitment, as mentioned, is crucial. Staff should have wide competencies and special powers, but these must be within the law. There should be substantial research capacity and the agency should be durable and ongoing.

ACAs operate across a spectrum from powerful effective bodies to ineffective. Sometimes they are a window through which one can

10.1057/9781137335098

see processes being improved, but sometimes they are just 'window dressing'.

Integrity systems

ACAs are agencies to which corruption can be reported, and which usually have included in their mandates some form of education and prevention. As shown above, not all public sector misbehaviour is necessarily corrupt, nor illegal. Sometimes there are examples of poor judgement, poor policy or lapses in acceptable behaviour. For an ACA to have any impact there need to be two fundamentals. There must be mechanisms and structures for government to be held accountable, and there must be a commitment to high standards of conduct for elected members and officials.

The ultimate accountability structure is the holding of free, fair and regular elections. There have been examples of elections being manipulated and rigged. Electoral malpractice has been systematically practiced in different types of regimes, and Sarah Birch describes and analyses the manipulation of electoral institutions, the manipulation of voter choice, the manipulation of electoral administration, all of which constitute corruption (Birch 2012). A comprehensive analysis of electoral corruption which covers examples from rural New York to Ohio and Texas in the United States, through to Guatemala, Colombia, Peru and Mexico has been conducted by Fabrice Lehoucq (2003). Systematic electoral corruption has followed the collapse of communism in 1989–90 in which electoral malpractice has become widespread, most notably in Belarus, Russia and the Ukraine (McAllister and White, 2011).

Integrity mechanisms in elections comprise one set of safeguards. Another is to have an audit office which is independent of the government of the day and which examines the management of public resources. A national audit office would conduct both financial and performance audits. Financially the auditor general would certify that financial statements genuinely reflect all transactions and accounts, and that income and expenditure has been undertaken in accordance with the law. Performance audits examine whether an agency is doing what it is supposed to be doing, doing it effectively and efficiently, and in a way as to achieve the agency's objectives as specified in law and to give good value for money. Most of what an auditor general would deal with is not the sort of corruption described in earlier chapters, though sometimes there may be fraud or deception. Corrupt behaviour and poor performance are sometimes intertwined and sometimes not.

An ombudsman, like an auditor general, should be independent of the government of the day. Complaints about decisions made by government agencies or about the conduct of their staff can come to the ombudsman who can investigate the process that led to a specific decision, or who can look more widely at systemic issues in decision making. Again, most of the matters referred to the ombudsman are not necessarily corrupt decisions, but rather decisions that do not follow process, sloppy or lazy behaviour by public officials or inappropriate acts by a government official which may victimize a client.

The best sign of organizational health and corruption resistance is an inbuilt acceptance that the agency insists on high standards of conduct from its employees. Rather than have big sticks for when standards are breached, agencies should build a strong culture of integrity that pervades the organization.

Many organizations publish integrity standards that start with the importance of agency culture, which includes values of integrity in process and communication and the building of ethical capacity. The next step is to ensure that operating strategies support this, that policies about behaviour are known and transparent, that risks can be assessed broadly and that if there is misconduct or corruption there is a sanction or treatment process.

We often find, standing alongside each other a code of ethics and a code of conduct. This essentially is a two-step process. First of all, the values of the organization are incorporated into an ethical code to assist members in understanding the difference between acceptable and unacceptable, or more bluntly between right and wrong. A written code identifies principles and standards that conform to organizational values, and is often a document expressed in abstract concepts. A code of conduct is more precise and prescriptive. It is often written in compliance terms, and sets out rules of practice and restrictions on behaviour. Many professions have a code of professional practice, which in essence is a code of conduct. A code of ethics sets up principles, and a code of conduct outlines behaviour. It must be noted, however that not every type of behaviour or risk can be anticipated, and rules cannot be written for every conceivable eventuality, and this is why ethical principles are important for guidance. In their perceptive book, *The Pursuit of Absolute*

10.1057/9781137335098

Integrity, Anechiarico and Jacobs (1996) show that implementation of severe codes of conduct do not necessarily lead to less corrupt practices.

A management environment which is built on integrity and morality needs to support this, and most important of all is the matter of leadership which demonstrates and practises morality and strong organizational integrity. The Corruption and Crime Commission of Western Australia is one of many agencies that have issued guidelines and checklists of how each of these can be assessed and achieved (CCC WA, 2008a).

The Western Australian guide sums up these issues in its opening statement:

> It is not enough to rely on legislation, codes of conduct and control systems to build a misconduct resistant agency. While it is important to express agency values in official communication, staff need to understand the real meaning of these values and see them applied in their workplace and in their leaders' behaviour.

In an early analysis of ethics measures in OECD countries, a comprehensive list is developed and analysed in each of its 29 countries. The most frequently stated core values in those countries' public documents (in order) were Legality, Integrity, Transparency, Efficiency, Equality, Responsibility, Justice and Impartiality (OECD, 2000, p. 32). However, these are values of such a high level that nobody would disagree much with them; and their implementation is much more difficult than their articulation. A more focused and targeted manageable analysis and set of checklists has recently been developed by the OECD. In its 2009 publication, *Towards a Sound Integrity Framework: Instruments, Processes, Structures and Conditions for Implementation*, analyses and practical examples are given throughout.

This OECD publication proposes an integrity management framework that is built on three pillars: Instruments, Processes and Structures. These have two layers, core measures and complementary measures. The core measures are specifically integrity oriented, such as conflict of interest codes, codes of ethics, integrity training and advice, whistleblowing arrangements, etc. The complementary measures are those that occur across the whole organization such as integrity as a criterion in personnel selection and promotion, recruitment and procurement processes (OECD, 2009, p. 22). The report goes on to provide guidelines on how to draft integrity codes, conflict of interest policies, post-public employment, enhancing integrity in public procurement, and many

10.1057/9781137335098

checklists on development and evaluation of the performance of these measures.

The development of an *integrity framework* can occur at many levels. To start with, questions such as the following might be asked:

▸ What are corruption risk areas?
▸ What opportunities are there for corrupt behaviour from both staff and other stakeholders?
▸ What controls are in place to identify and manage these risks?
▸ Are they adequate? Why and how so?
▸ Do these controls integrate with the agency's goals?
▸ What pushback, indifference or other resistance is there – or would you expect – by staff on compliance processes?
▸ Are there enough resources to identify and cover these risks, and are the systems robust enough to meet the challenges if the risks are realized?
▸ Are there operating procedures and codes of conduct?
▸ Are at-risk staff trained to conduct themselves appropriately?
▸ Are there adequate arrangements to report confidentially and safely?

These would be assessed against a backdrop of structures:

▸ Top management oversight;
▸ Allocation of responsibility;
▸ Education and training;
▸ Regular communications designed to secure compliance;
▸ Monitoring systems;
▸ Reporting systems.

Analysing risk and developing preventive strategies becomes a major classification task. Some business activities involve more corruption risk than others. On pages 37–38 above we listed some of the most obvious risks in administration which have been identified by Angela Gorta (2006).

Understanding which risks apply in an agency is the first step in building an integrity framework. The second is assessing the risks for the agency from their key functions, the third is developing mitigation and control strategies that suit an agency's risk profile and operations, and fourth is motivating staff to want this done and done well. The best compliance comes from staff who see the need for it and are committed to doing it.

10.1057/9781137335098

What is very obvious is that not all agencies might need to, nor be able to, develop a gold-standard integrity framework. If they choose to develop at a lower standard, the risks and limitations should be understood.

International attempts to combat corruption

As corruption becomes global, so too do the efforts to control and combat it. There are many international agreements that form part of the architecture, and some parts of these are oriented to anti-corruption agencies, while other parts of these agreements focus on events and activities of corruption. Table 4.1 gives details of some of these agreements.

TABLE 4.1   *Treaties and international arrangements*

Treaties

United Nations Convention against Corruption (UNCAC)	http://www.unodc.org/unodc/en/treaties/CAC/index.html
OECD Convention on Combating Bribery of Foreign Public Officials in International Business Transactions	http://www.oecd.org/corruption/oecdantibriberyconvention.htm
Council of Europe's Criminal Law Convention on Corruption	http://conventions.coe.int/Treaty/Commun/QueVoulezVous.asp?CL=ENG&NT=173
Additional Protocol to the Council of Europe's Criminal Law Convention on Corruption	http://www.conventions.coe.int/Treaty/Commun/QueVoulezVous.asp?NT=191&CM=8&DF=02/05/2013&CL=ENG
Council of Europe's Civil Law Convention on Corruption	http://conventions.coe.int/Treaty/Commun/QueVoulezVous.asp?NT=174&CL=ENG
G20 Anti-Corruption Working Group	http://www.g20civil.com/documents/195/364/
Asia-Pacific Economic Cooperation (APEC) Anti-Corruption and Transparency Task Force (2004)	http://www.apec.org/Groups/SOM-Steering-Committee-on-Economic-and-Technical-Cooperation/Working-Groups/Anti-Corruption-and-Transparency.aspx
Official bodies	
World Bank	http://web.worldbank.org/
Asian Development Bank* (ADB)	http://www.adb.org
Civil society	
Transparency International	http://www.transparency.org/\
U4 Anti-Corruption Resource Centre	http://www.u4.no
Global Witness	http://www.globalwitness.org
Other items of interest	

Continued

TABLE 4.1   *Continued*

Treaties	
1996 Inter-American Convention against Corruption of the Organization of American States	http://www.oas.org/juridico/english/treaties/b-58.html
African Union Convention 2003 (the 2003 African Union Convention on Preventing and Combating Corruption)	http://www.africa-union.org/official_documents/Treaties_%20Conventions_%20Protocols/Convention%20on%20Combating%20Corruption.pdf
GRECO (the 1999 Criminal Law Convention on Corruption and the 1999 Civil Law Convention on Corruption of the Council of Europe)	http://conventions.coe.int/Treaty/en/Treaties/Html/174.htm http://conventions.coe.int/Treaty/en/Treaties/Html/173.htm
Asia Pacific Group on Money Laundering (1997)	http://www.apgml.org/about/history.aspx
Financial Action Task Force (FATF, 1989)	http://www.fatf-gafi.org/pages/aboutus/
ADB-OECD Anti-Corruption Initiative (1999)	http://www.oecd.org/site/adboecdanti-corruptioninitiative/

The United Nations Convention against Corruption

The most comprehensive is the United Nations Convention against Corruption (UNCAC). It entered into force in December 2005, and by 2013, 165 state parties had signed on to the treaty. It is the first and most widely agreed to global mechanism for the control of corruption, though there are some notable exceptions. While, perhaps unsurprisingly, Chad, South Sudan, North Korea and Somalia are not signatories, Japan, New Zealand and Germany to date have not ratified the treaty, though they have signed it.

Once a country has signed the treaty, this signals an agreement to its objectives and a willingness to put in place the mechanisms required in the treaty; and once ratified, this signals that those mechanisms are (or at least should be) in place. The purposes of the UNCAC are:

1   to promote and strengthen measures to prevent and combat corruption more efficiently and effectively;
2   to promote, facilitate and support international co-operation and technical assistance in the prevention of and fight against corruption, including in asset recovery;
3   to promote integrity, accountability and proper management of public affairs and public property.

The UNCAC introduces standards, measures and rules that all countries can apply in order to strengthen their legal and regulatory regimes to fight corruption. It also calls for preventive measures and the criminalization of the most prevalent forms of corruption in both public and private sectors. Lastly, UNCAC requires member states to return assets obtained through corruption to the country from which they were stolen. A range of related technical tools and publications are available on the UNODC website: http://www.unodc.org/unodc/en/corruption/publications.html. The official documentation from the UN outlines the key features of the UNCAC, and these are reproduced here from http://www.unodc.org/unodc/en/treaties/CAC/index.html.

Prevention

It is noted that corruption can be prosecuted after the fact, but nonetheless first and foremost, it requires prevention. Article 5 of the Convention enjoins each state party to establish and promote effective practices aimed at the prevention of corruption.

These include model preventive policies, such as the establishment of anti-corruption bodies and enhanced transparency in the financing of election campaigns and political parties. States must endeavour to ensure that their public services are subject to safeguards that promote efficiency, transparency and recruitment based on merit. Once recruited, public officials should be subject to codes of conduct, requirements for financial and other disclosures, and appropriate disciplinary measures. Transparency and accountability in matters of public finance must also be promoted, and specific requirements are established for the prevention of corruption, in the particularly critical areas of the public sector, such as the judiciary and public procurement. Those who use public services must expect a high standard of conduct from their public officials.

Preventing public corruption also requires an effort from all members of society at large. For these reasons, the Convention calls on countries to promote actively the involvement of non-governmental and community-based organizations, as well as other elements of civil society, and to raise public awareness of corruption and what can be done about it.

10.1057/9781137335098

Criminalization

The Convention requires countries to establish criminal and other offences to cover a wide range of acts of corruption, if these are not already crimes under domestic law. In some cases, states are legally obliged to establish offences; in other cases, in order to take into account differences in domestic law, they are required to consider doing so. The Convention goes beyond previous instruments of this kind, calling not only for the criminalization of basic forms of corruption such as bribery and the embezzlement of public funds, but also for consideration of the criminalization of trading in influence and the concealment and laundering of the proceeds of corruption. Offences committed in support of corruption, including money-laundering and obstructing justice, are also dealt with.

International co-operation

Countries agreed to co-operate with one another in every aspect of the fight against corruption, including prevention, investigation and the prosecution of offenders. Countries are bound by the Convention to render specific forms of mutual legal assistance in gathering and transferring evidence for use in court, to extradite offenders. Countries are also required to undertake measures which will support the tracing, freezing, seizure and confiscation of the proceeds of corruption.

Asset recovery

In a major breakthrough, countries agreed on asset recovery, which is stated explicitly as a fundamental principle of the Convention. This is a particularly important issue for many developing countries where high-level corruption has plundered the national wealth, and where resources are badly needed for reconstruction and the rehabilitation of societies under new governments. Several provisions specify how co-operation and assistance will be rendered. In particular, in the case of embezzlement of public funds, the confiscated property would be returned to the state requesting it.

Effective asset-recovery provisions will support the efforts of countries to redress the worst effects of corruption, while sending at the same time a message to corrupt officials that there will be no place to hide

10.1057/9781137335098

their illicit assets. Accordingly, article 51 provides for the return of assets to countries of origin as a fundamental principle of this Convention. Article 43 obliges state parties to extend the widest possible co-operation to each other in the investigation and prosecution of offences defined in the Convention.

The programme is ambitious and there has been criticism from many who argue not only that the UNCAC has not been effective but, worse than that, has little likelihood of succeeding. These critics point out that countries that rank near the bottom of the Transparency International Corruption Perception Index, such as Afghanistan, Uzbekistan, Iraq, Venezuela and Haiti, have all ratified the UNCAC, and some have done so with great haste. Kenya, which ranks 139 out of 174 on the TI CPI index, signed and ratified the Convention on the same day, while other countries which do poorly on the rankings, such as Belarus, Algeria, Honduras, Mexico and Nigeria, all ratified in less than a year after signing. The implication is that for at least some, if not many, of these countries, the signature and ratification of UNCAC was regarded almost as a formality, without any serious political commitment to seeing what legislative, policy and practical changes are actually needed.

UNCAC evaluation

Evaluating the effectiveness of something like the UNCAC is a slow and exhausting process. While negotiating the treaty was complex and drawn out, establishing a review mechanism was also very time consuming. Richer, Western countries wanted an 'open review' process in which independent experts would gather information and write a report. The poorer countries were reluctant to let this happen; many thought it would be a means by which donor countries could criticize aid recipients and countries which did not apply 'Western' values to legislation and the rule of law. Instead they advocated a 'controlled review' process in which government information would be made available to expert reviewers, who would include in their number people from the country being reviewed. A compromise was eventually reached (see Joutsen & Graycar, 2012). The first review results should become available from 2014.

10.1057/9781137335098

Alina Mungiu-Pippidi and her colleagues (2011) caution against hasty judgements. They point out that after less than a decade it is unrealistic to expect that great progress could be made against so apparently intractable an issue. They note that less than a decade after the 1948 adoption of the Universal Declaration of Human Rights, only a handful of countries were considered to be compliant. Even 60 years later only less than half of the world's countries could be regarded as compliant, and these represent 43 per cent of the global population. While progress is being made slowly, 57 per cent of the world's population live in countries where human rights cannot be assumed. Any assumption that corruption control will flow immediately because the UNCAC is in force is naïve.

With UNCAC, however, a norm has been set and formal agreement to the goals is nearly universal. This sets the stage for putting in place formal domestic strategies. As Mungiu-Pippidi notes, 'UNCAC is a collection of institutional tools, not all similarly effective or useful of which some have the potential to become effective weapons' (2011, p. xvi).

OECD Convention

The OECD Convention on Combating Bribery of Foreign Public Officials in International Business Transactions came into effect in February 1999. Ratified by 34 OECD countries and six non-member countries (Argentina, Brazil, Bulgaria, Colombia, Russia and South Africa) it is a mechanism by which 40 countries have agreed to put in place new measures that will reinforce their efforts to prevent, detect and investigate foreign bribery.

The convention establishes legally binding standards in order to criminalize bribery of foreign public officials in international business transactions, and provides for related measures that make this effective. It is the only international anti-corruption instrument focused on the 'supply side' of the bribery transaction. Parties commit themselves to ensuring that their national parliaments approve the Convention and pass legislation necessary for its implementation into domestic law. It also permits countries to move in a co-ordinated manner to adopt national legislation that makes it a crime to bribe foreign public officials.

10.1057/9781137335098

The Convention provides a broad definition of bribery, requiring countries to impose dissuasive sanctions and committing them to providing mutual legal assistance.

Council of Europe

The Council of Europe has both a criminal law convention on corruption and a civil law convention on corruption. The criminal convention, which has been ratified by 45 countries and came into effect in 2002, develops common standards concerning certain corruption offences. It also deals with substantive and procedural law matters, which relate to these corruption offences and seek to improve international co-operation. It does not provide a uniform definition of corruption. The civil convention which came into effect in 2003 requires countries to provide in their domestic law for effective remedies for persons who have suffered damage as a result of acts of corruption, in order to enable them to defend their rights and interests, including the possibility of obtaining compensation for damage.

G20

The most recent international anti-corruption structure is the G20 Anti-Corruption Working Group. This does not have any real status, since the G20 is only a dialogue forum. Nevertheless, the G20 has a special responsibility to fight corruption because it represents 85 per cent of the global economy and two-thirds of the world's population. G20 countries are duty-bound to develop effective structures to promote a transparent economic environment and, in addition, encourage growth. The main task of the Working Group is to have full implementation of the UNCAC by member countries in support largely of a clean business environment.

To prevent corrupt officials from accessing the global financial system and from laundering their proceeds of corruption, the G20 has set up agreements for the recovery of stolen assets, especially those protected by bank secrecy. All G20 countries will adopt measures related to preventing and detecting transfers of proceeds of crime; measures for direct recovery of property; mechanisms for recovery of property through international co-operation in asset tracing, freezing and confiscation; measures for special co-operation in voluntary disclosure; and return and disposal of assets.

To prevent corrupt officials from being able to travel abroad with impunity, G20 countries will consider a co-operative framework to deny entry and safe haven in their jurisdictions to corrupt officials, and those who corrupt them. To that end, G20 experts will work towards denying visas to corrupt people. For example, the Prime Minister of Papua New Guinea claimed that he had been informed by the Australian government that Australia will no longer issue visas to PNG citizens who are alleged to have bought properties or invested in Australia using money gained through corrupt means (reported on ABC Radio Australia, 3 November 2012).

The main task of the G20 countries has been to support the revision of the standards of the Financial Action Task Force (FATF) and publish information about how to request legal assistance and recover misappropriated assets at the national level. The G20 has also agreed on principles for financial and asset disclosure of public officials.

Other mechanisms

There are other mechanisms such as the Asia-Pacific Economic Cooperation (APEC) Anti-Corruption and Transparency Task Force; the 1996 Inter-American Convention against Corruption of the Organization of American States; the African Union Convention 2003 (the 2003 African Union Convention on Preventing and Combating Corruption); the Asia Pacific Group on Money Laundering (1997); the Financial Action Task Force (FATF, 1989); the ADB-OECD Anti-Corruption Initiative (1999). These and others can be searched for on the internet.

Civil society

Non-government organizations play a significant role in corruption control as activists and advocates, information providers and critics, whistleblowers and support groups. Generally described as civil society, these groups participate right across the spectrum from

10.1057/9781137335098

assisting with data and policy input to severe and trenchant criticism of poor practice. They can be found in every corner of the globe. Sometimes they are reviled and disparaged by governments, and at other times cautiously tolerated. The most prominent is Transparency International. TI, as it is often known, was established in 1993 to build effective measures to tackle corruption. It is a politically non-partisan organization with an international secretariat in Berlin and more than 100 national chapters worldwide, each registered in their own countries as independent civil society organizations. TI is a non-profit, non-governmental organization and the majority of its income comes from government development agency budgets and foundations. It is highly active in projects, information and advocacy, and a great deal of information can be found on its website http://transparency.org.

U4, based in Norway, is a private social science research foundation working on issues of development and human rights. It was established in 2002 as an initiative of the ministers of international development from the Netherlands, Germany, Norway and the UK, though other countries have since become funding partners. U4 operates a resource centre which provides relevant information and services to its partner agencies, and Transparency International in Berlin is responsible for the U4 Help Desk. The U4 Anti-Corruption Resource Centre assists donor practitioners to more effectively address corruption challenges through their development support. Its Issues Papers, Expert Answers, Briefing Papers and Practice Insights are available on its website http://www.u4.no.

Some NGOs are more focused. Global Witness for example, runs pioneering campaigns against natural-resource-related conflict and corruption and associated environmental and human rights abuses. Established in the UK in 1993, it is a not-for-profit organization whose objectives include preventing natural resource companies from acting corruptly or enabling corruption in countries where they operate; preventing the financial system from enabling resource-related corruption; curbing the ability of public officials to loot their state's funds; and ensuring that governments do not enable or legitimize corruption. It runs a variety of campaigns and in-depth investigations. More information can be found at http://www.globalwitness.org.

The quest for integrity and anti-corruption is a monumental struggle. It is not simply a matter of writing a code of conduct or some laws

10.1057/9781137335098

making corruption illegal. As Mungiu-Pippidi argues, the whole exercise is confounded by conceptual flaws, imprecise measurement and inadequate strategies. The quest, globally, is really a series of national and domestic battles fought on domestic battlefields in which in poorer countries predatory elites battle with losers, and in richer countries people with power, even petty power, use monopoly positions without accountability to seek unfair rents.

10.1057/9781137335098

5

Applying Crime Prevention and Regulatory Theory to Corruption

Abstract: *This chapter builds on the framework outlined in the previous chapter by adopting a more specific theoretical approach to designing effective corruption prevention strategies. The chapter first highlights the relevance of situational crime prevention. This is supported by an analysis of regulatory theory, especially the idea of 'smart regulation', and the application of TASP diagnostics. These approaches converge around the idea of a process of (1) analysis of specific corruption types, (2) development of interventions and (3) testing of interventions using triangulated corruption indicators. Examples are provided of particular types of corruption opportunity reducing measures. The chapter concludes by focusing on the role of 'big gun' anti-corruption commissions.*

Graycar, Adam and Prenzler, Tim. *Understanding and Preventing Corruption*. Basingstoke: Palgrave Macmillan, 2013. DOI: 10.1057/9781137335098.

10.1057/9781137335098

Depending on the nature of the specific corruption and the context of corruption as described in earlier chapters, prevention can occur at many levels. The previous chapter discussed the architecture of broad controls by the use of legislative, organizational and international structures. This chapter develops some theoretical underpinnings to prevention, taking lessons from situational crime prevention (SCP) and regulatory theory. SCP helps us understand how to examine and prevent corrupt events. Regulatory theory focuses on guardianship and supports a 'big gun' approach to corruption prevention.

Of course, these approaches are complementary to practices within organizations that build integrity standards and codes, educate participants and stakeholders in ethical behaviour, protect whistleblowers within an organization and outside (such as the media), as well as strengthen integrity and independence of the major institutions in any society, such as legislatures, the judiciary, audit offices, the civil service and the police.

As we have seen in this book so far, efforts to detect and prevent corruption are often ad hoc. Consequently, they are also often hit and miss in their impacts. Common sources on corruption prevention – mainly government agencies and NGOs – tend not to have clear theoretical positions about best-practice approaches. This chapter sets out an approach to corruption prevention which is more systematic and theoretically informed. In particular, it provides a set of approaches to prevention based on two key areas of knowledge: situational crime prevention and regulatory theory. These approaches are developed from the themes in Chapter 2 on understanding corruption, particularly the emphasis on opportunity, along with the TASP approach. The focus is on opportunity-reducing techniques, 'smart regulation' and the potential benefits of 'big gun' anti-corruption commissions.

Theoretical frameworks

Situational crime prevention (SCP) has provided the most important framework internationally for developing effective crime-prevention strategies, and it can also be used for corruption prevention. It involves the introduction of measures designed to foreclose opportunities in the location – or situation – in which offences occur. Clarke (1997, p. 6) refers to four components of the framework:

10.1057/9781137335098

1   A theoretical foundation drawing principally upon routine activity and rational choice approaches;
2   A standard methodology based on the action research paradigm;
3   A set of opportunity-reducing techniques; and
4   A body of evaluated practice including studies of displacement.

Furthermore,

> Situational prevention comprises opportunity-reducing measures that (1) are directed at highly specific forms of crime, (2) involve the management, design or manipulation of the immediate environment in as systematic and permanent way as possible, (3) make crime more difficult and risky, or less rewarding and excusable as judged by a wide range of offenders. (Clarke, 1997, p. 4)

Cornish and Clarke (2003) break down this approach into a matrix of 25 specific techniques, a number of which are particularly relevant to corruption, grouped under five 'purposes':

▶ increase the effort;
▶ increase the risks;
▶ reduce the rewards;
▶ reduce provocations;
▶ remove excuses.

There is evidence demonstrating major reductions in crime using these techniques. For example, in *Situational Crime Prevention: Successful Case Studies*, Clarke (1997) reproduced 23 accounts of effective crime reduction. These include deterring obscene phone callers by reducing anonymity using caller ID, reducing subway graffiti by removing rewards through rapid cleaning and reducing retail theft by screening exits via electronic article surveillance.

Two case studies in Clarke's book relate to corruption. One focuses on reduction of cheque fraud in Sweden. Until the 1970s, banks and retailers would allow, without identification, the cashing of cheques up to a limit of 300 kroner. This facilitated business but it created a perfect opportunity for fraud. Banks and retailers were reluctant to change, as it involved more processes; but when identification became a required feature, offences fell by 86 per cent. An 'expensive and ineffective system of formal control' – through complex police investigations and prosecutions – was largely superseded by 'an inexpensive and effective situational control' based on reducing anonymity (Knutsson & Kuhlhorn, 1997, p. 116).

10.1057/9781137335098

In the second study, Kuhlhorn (1997) evaluated the impact of data-matching on fraud in housing subsidies. A computerized system identified discrepancies between income estimates for recipients of subsidized housing and recipients of sickness insurance. The first group was tempted to understate their income in order to increase their housing subsidy, the second to overstate their income to increase their sickness benefit. In the first year, a pilot run resulted in 39,408 households losing all or part of their housing subsidy. Further savings were achieved with more specific data-matching parameters. The ability to cross-reference databases reduced the opportunity to cheat by increasing formal surveillance and improving access control.

An important point about SCP is that the famous matrix of 25 techniques works best as a guide to thinking about ways of solving crime problems – rather than providing off-the-shelf solutions to crime or corruption problems. Finding the most effective techniques is best achieved through an 'action research' paradigm. 'Action' refers to practitioner-researcher collaboration and the involvement of stakeholders in an applied-research process. In that regard, Clarke (1997, p. 15) sets out five stages required for the implementation of a situational prevention project:

1 Collection of data about the nature and dimensions of the specific crime problem;
2 Analysis of the situational conditions that permit or facilitate the commission of the crime in question;
3 Systematic study of possible means of blocking opportunities for these particular crimes, including analysis of costs;
4 Implementation of the most promising, feasible and economic measures;
5 Monitoring of results and dissemination of experience.

Consistent pre- and post-intervention measures of crime problems are therefore essential. As we know, however, measurement of corruption is problematic, with only limited reliance on reported corruption. Nonetheless, as Chapter 3 has shown, there are ways of obtaining estimates for corruption; and reliability is enhanced through triangulating as many methods as possible.

Regulatory theory provides another body of knowledge relevant to corruption prevention. Crime prevention is usually concerned with eliminating a behaviour – such as robbery or theft. Regulation, on the other hand,

10.1057/9781137335098

is often concerned with allowing an activity to occur while minimizing unfair practices and harmful side effects. A primary focus is the regulation of business activity by government agencies; and business–government transactions are, of course, a key area for corruption. Numerous studies have been conducted on how governments regulate industries like banking and investment services, manufacturing and retail. Regulatory failure has been a recurring theme. Explanations include inadequate legal powers, inadequate resourcing of regulators, institutional cultures of deference and 'capture' of regulators by regulated industries – including through friendships, sharing of personnel and bribery.

In their aptly titled and timeless book, *Of Manners Gentle: Enforcement Strategies of Australian Business Regulatory Agencies*, Grabosky and Braithwaite (1986, pp. 222–229) set out a typology of regulatory agencies, with each type describing factors involved in under-regulation and regulatory failure:

1 'Conciliators' eschew prosecution and seek to improve compliance by facilitating dialogue and mutual agreements between complainants and accused companies;
2 'Benign big guns...walk softly while carrying a very big stick' (p. 224), rarely using their considerable powers;
3 'Diagnostic inspectorates' value good relations and provide expert advice, avoiding confrontation and encouraging self-regulation;
4 'Detached token enforcers' tend not to value good relations yet engage in only limited enforcement;
5 'Detached modest enforcers' are also largely unconcerned about good relations, but are sticklers for the rules and engage in more activity;
6 'Token enforcers' initiate a steady flow of prosecutions, but the prosecutions result in only light penalties with little deterrent effect;
7 'Modest enforcers' score the highest on enforcement activity and average sanctions, and also make better use of 'alternative means of enforcement: licence suspensions, shutting down production, injunctions, and adverse publicity'. (p. 226)

Since the publication of *Of Manners Gentle* there has been an evolution of regulatory theory describing and advocating more effective approaches, including 'responsive regulation' (Ayres & Braithwaite, 1992), 'smart regulation' (Gunningham & Grabosky, 1998) and 'regulatory craftsmanship' (Sparrow, 2000b). Within these frameworks, researchers

10.1057/9781137335098

have argued that effective regulation occurs through attention to a 'regulatory mix' and an *'enforcement pyramid'*. The core argument is that compliance is most likely to be achieved when regulators (a) have a wide range of enforcement strategies available to them and (b) find the right mix of strategies.

Braithwaite's enforcement pyramid involves six levels: 'License Revocation, License Suspension, Criminal Penalty, Civil Penalty, Warning Letter, Persuasion' (Ayres & Braithwaite, 1992, p. 35). Placing strategies in a hierarchy allows regulators to select those most likely to be effective in different circumstances, and to escalate levels of enforcement when lower levels fail. One example provided within the regulation literature is the Boston Gun Project, initiated in 1995, which led to an immediate 68 per cent reduction in youth homicides, followed by ongoing reductions (Sparrow, 2000b, ch. 12). Detailed research led to the development of two-pronged, multi-agency strategy. Communication with gangs included warnings of intensive law enforcement and heavy penalties. If the warnings were ignored, authorities followed up with saturation enforcement, thereby reinforcing the messages in the communication strategy. Similar examples can be found in industry where companies undertake initial voluntary compliance before government controls come into effect (Gunningham & Grabosky, 1998).

Each regulatory strategy comes with advantages and costs or risks that should be estimated before implementation. For example, shutting down a corruptly established polluting factory might cause severe hardship through unemployment and non-availability of a product. Responsive regulation also entails communication and consultation. Regulated industries are a potential source of valuable ideas and expertise. While regulators need to guard against capture, they should also avoid unilateral anti-corruption measures that might be ineffectual or provoke resistance.

Applications to corruption

Application of the SCP framework to corruption has a great deal of potential to strengthen and extend the range of available anti-corruption measures. For example, the Swedish fraud-reduction case studies outlined above have a number of implications for preventing corrupt public sector payment fraud related to increasing effort, increasing formal surveillance and reducing anonymity. A system of approvals involving more than one person will help stop public servants making illicit payments to themselves or their cronies. The principle of 'double signing' of payments assists in this process, especially if second or subsequent signatures are required at higher management levels. Of course, productivity losses should be considered.

Data-matching has also been extended enormously since these studies, and can be used to compare individuals' legal income against their account holdings and assets, and deter corruption and fraud as well as prevent money laundering. The related area of transaction reporting also provides a means of flagging possible illegal payments. These strategies involve improved guardianship, surveillance and entry/exit screening.

A situational approach has also been applied to corruption in more developed applied studies. In 'Situational Corruption Prevention', Ede et al. (2002) tested the hypothesis that situational crime prevention techniques would be useful in preventing police corruption. The researchers first developed a theoretical set of prevention strategies by integrating the police corruption and situational prevention literatures. A summary of the results is shown in Table 5.1, covering 11 techniques which are subsets of the 25-cell matrix which can be found at http://www.popcenter.org/25techniques/.

The researchers then undertook a situational analysis of police complaints files, using three years of substantiated cases in Queensland, Australia. The complaints were officially deemed 'corruption' by the state's anti-corruption commission. Situational prevention techniques were found to be relevant to complaints involving 'misuse of authority for a reward' or 'a breach of criminal law'. The sample included 174 complaint files, involving 213 allegations, across the categories 'opportunistic thefts', 'driving under the influence of alcohol', 'assault (while off-duty)' and 'theft from employer'.

The researchers were unable to develop a classic intervention project. However, the exercise was consistent with the first key step in situational prevention: analysis of situational variables. The analysis demonstrated the potential for developing practical and often simple methods for reducing or closing off corruption opportunities. The opportunistic theft cases appeared particularly amenable to situational interventions. These are reported in Table 5.2. The categories covered conduct officially deemed corruption largely by virtue of being crimes. There were very few cases involving graft, but the researchers concluded that better record

TABLE 5.1   *Police anti-corruption strategies containing a situational component*

Technique	Description
Target hardening	Strategies designed to increase the security of drugs, cash or other property seized by police
Deflecting offenders	Removing arrest quotas which place a priority on quantity over quality and pressure police to fabricate evidence
	Compulsory rotation, on the assumption that it takes time to develop the ties necessary for most corruption
Controlling facilitators	Computer audit trails to reduce the incidence of the misuse of police computer information facilities
Entry screening	Recruitment procedures such as the inclusion of background investigations, tests of emotional and psychological fitness, probationary periods for recruits
Formal surveillance	Strategies to increase effective supervision, such as management accountability, making it part of the commander's role to seek out and eliminate corrupt activities among their personnel
	Integrity testing which purposely places officers in potentially compromising positions and monitors their resulting behaviour
	Establishing an external oversight body to investigate police and carry out physical surveillance to increase perceived risks of detection
Surveillance by employees	Protections and rewards for whistleblowers and informers
	Field associates (police officers, usually recently graduated recruits) recruited to secretly report any corruption they observe during the course of their regular duties
Natural surveillance by the public	Strategies to encourage complaints, such as easy-to-access complaints systems
Reducing temptation	Eliminate police policies of discretionary enforcement for minor offences likely to give rise to corruption problems (for example, speeding, drink driving, prostitution)
Rule setting	Strategies to instil professionalism via a detailed explicit code of ethics
	Tightening regulations governing situations likely to give rise to allegations of corruption, such as strict procedures for dealing with seized money and drugs; systems for the registration of informants; and policies of requiring two people to be present during meetings with informants, counting money and male–female encounters
Identifying property	Marking or tracing of drugs, cash or other property seized by police
Denying benefits	The 'exclusionary rule' (where judges disallow evidence obtained illegally by police)

Source: Ede et al., p. 213. Used with the permission of Federation Press.

10.1057/9781137335098

keeping and larger samples could lead to the identification of more situational measures that could be taken against classic corruption.

The essence of a situational approach is to understand and identify opportunities and ensure that a 'capable guardian' is in place. This approach, demonstrated in relation to police corruption in Table 5.2, can be applied in other public sector settings where there are risks of

TABLE 5.2   *Opportunity-reducing techniques derived from theft findings*

Target hardening	Establish minimum standards throughout the police service for the storage of money (even social funds) and other valuables (including firearms)
Access control	Reduce number of officers with access to money storage
Strengthening moral condemnation	Cashbox stickers: 'Only a dog steals from mates'
	On forms: 'Claiming for time you did not work is stealing', 'Check dates as false claims will result in departmental action'
	On pay-slips: 'Paid work while on sick leave is stealing'
	Similar warning on Workers' Compensation Board payments
Surveillance by employees	Rotation of treasurers to prevent long periods where one person sees the books
	Policies ensuring dual responsibility (two signatures) for monies paid out and requiring the presence of another officer when counting or moving money or valuables
Formal surveillance	More regular checks on books, claim forms and police property in the possession of officers
	More stock-takes of goods and property storage facilities
	Placing the onus for loss upon managers to ensure that checks and stocktakes are conducted thoroughly
Target removal	More frequent banking would have prevented the large loss suffered by the Police Club
Identifying property	The marking of police property clearly and permanently with the 'QPS' initials may deter theft of property for private use
Rule setting	Educating officers in the rules for claiming travel allowances and training officers acting in positions with book-keeping responsibility
	More onus to comply with existing rules via the use of sanctions for failing to comply and rewards (such as supervisor recognition) for following procedures
	Establish rules where none or poor ones exist (for example, in many book-keeping areas and in regard to the use of police property by officers over long time periods)
Facilitating compliance	The provision of an in-house financial consultant available for appointments or telephone advice
	Paying officers for overtime, as unpaid overtime can result in the temptation to obtain payment via corrupt means
	Making forms easier to complete, for example, by redesign and printing calculation rates on them

Source: Adapted from Ede et al., 2002, p. 222. Used with the permission of Federation Press.

10.1057/9781137335098

corruption. Examples of target personnel include customs or immigration officials, officers who issue permits and licences, people who carry out inspections such as health inspectors or water inspectors, people who issue welfare benefits, people who approve town planning applications, and many more.

It is necessary to find the most effective mix of strategies to minimize corruption. In many cases this will include a 'big gun' agency, with adequate resources and legal powers to counter entrenched resistance to corruption laws. Anti-corruption commissions, as described in Chapter 4, have emerged over the past 40 years as the big guns of corruption control. As with any regulatory agency, they run the risk of serving as 'tokenistic enforcers'. However, there is evidence that they can be highly effective through situational techniques of extending guardianship, strengthening formal surveillance, disrupting markets, denying benefits, alerting conscience and discouraging imitation. The following sections outline developments in this area with two case studies of Hong Kong and Australia.

The Hong Kong ICAC

The Hong Kong ICAC is considered the pioneering public sector-wide – or omnibus – integrity agency – although it is unusual in also covering the private sector. From the beginning, the Commission was characterized by statutory independence, the recruitment of outside and specialist investigators to support independence and competency, a large staff to address the large scale of the problem, and a culture of investigative and prosecutorial zeal (ICAC Hong Kong, 2011; see also Chapter 4). In one of its early, high-profile, successes, the Commission shut down a scam in which traffic police received routine payments for ignoring traffic violations by commercial vehicles.

The ICAC's regulatory mix has included an enormous and sustained public education campaign, which encourages public disclosures. Whistleblower protections contributed to an environment of trust for complainants. Outreach is enhanced through seven regional offices. The Commission engages in covert surveillance, forensic accounting, and proactive inspections and auditing; and it has significant powers of search and seizure, and powers to compel testimony (Heilbrunn, 2004; Scott, 2011b) It has a highly developed programme for assisting public and private entities to develop their own corruption-prevention programmes.

This work is supported by legislation that is seen as comprehensive in clearly articulating a wide range of corruption-related offences – including the Elections (Corrupt and Illegal Conduct) Ordinance and Prevention of Bribery Ordinance. Between 1974 and 1985, prosecutions averaged 300 persons per year. In the peak year of 2000, approximately 600 persons were prosecuted on corruption charges and 100 cautioned. In 2011, prosecutions were mounted against 283 persons and 54 were cautioned. In the same year, complaints against persons in government made up the minority of complaints (28 per cent) and prosecutions (7 per cent) (ICAC Hong Kong, 2012, pp. 10, 30 & 85–86).

The Commission also attracts extremely high levels of public confidence. The most recent survey, for 2011, included the following findings (p. 68):

> Almost all survey respondents considered that the ICAC deserved their support (98 per cent) and that keeping Hong Kong corruption-free is important to the overall development of Hong Kong (99.2 per cent). A vast majority of the respondents (87.8 per cent) considered ICAC's anticorruption work effective. Public tolerance of corruption remained low. Using a 0 to 10 rating scale, of which 0 represents total rejection and 10 total tolerance of corruption, the mean score for 2011 was 0.7, the lowest recorded over the years, reflecting a very low level of tolerance of corruption amongst the survey respondents. Moreover, the majority of the respondents (77.2 per cent) said they were willing to report corruption.

In addition, 71.2 per cent of respondents considered corruption 'uncommon' in Hong Kong, and 98.5 per cent said they had not 'come across corruption' in the preceding year (ICAC Hong Kong, 2011 p. vii).

These results seem almost too good to be true and ICAC's operations have often been controversial. However, the Commission is widely considered to have made a major contribution to Hong Kong's image of integrity (Heilbrunn, 2004). Hong Kong has received consistently high scores since it was ranked on the TI Corruption Perceptions Index. In 2012, out of 176 countries or territories, it was ranked 14th (Transparency International, 2012, p. 3). In 2011, Hong Kong was ranked in the 94.3 percentile for 'control of corruption' by the World Bank (2012), up from 92.7 in 2002.

This is a remarkable achievement, sustained after Hong Kong returned to the sovereignty of China's corrupt Communist Party in 1997. In 2012,

China ranked 80 in the TI survey, with a score of 39. Apart from retaining the ICAC, Hong Kong also has partial independence from China through a limited democracy, and it retains a reputation for an independent judiciary (Scott, 2011a; U4, 2010).

Australian integrity commissions

Australia is another location where there has been considerable development in the area of public sector-wide integrity commissions. For much of its history Australia relied on traditional pillars of government accountability – including the separation of powers, free media, ombudsmen and auditor generals (Brown & Head, 2005).

Ombudsmen were introduced from the 1970s, primarily to deal with complaints about administrative decisions, some of which might entail corruption. Police were expected to deal with corruption of a criminal nature. However, many police departments were deeply corrupt and themselves the subjects of numerous complaints. Growing distrust of internal investigations and recurring high-profile scandals drove a strong trend towards the establishment of powerful commissions, referred to as 'standing royal commissions' (Prenzler, 2011). The argument was that the powers of *ad hoc* royal commissions – such as subpoena powers – underpinned their success in revealing corruption and needed to be retained to maintain reform.

Australia also ranks as a very low-corruption country in the Transparency International Corruption Perception Index – equal 7th in 2012, though one can debate whether this is due to the big guns of various anti-corruption agencies which now exist in every state (though some have longer histories than others). Public opinion surveys conducted by and for the ACAs generally show strong public support. For example, in Western Australia, a 2008 survey (CCC WA 2008b, pp. 12 & 17) found that:

▶ 98.4 per cent of respondents agreed with the statement 'I feel that it is a good thing to have a body like the Triple C';
▶ 97.6 per cent agreed with the statement 'I feel that it is important for a body like the Triple C to be independent from government, i.e. not under direct influence or control but accountable to parliament';
▶ 80.2 per cent said that if they were to make a complaint to the commission they felt confident that it would 'properly investigate' the complaint.

In Queensland, a 2011 survey (CMC QLD, pp. 19, 21, 31 & 35) found that:

- 90 per cent of respondents agreed with the statement 'Complaints about public service employees should be investigated by an oversight body, not by the government';
- 85 per cent believed 'public service employees generally behave well' and 81 per cent believed 'most public service employees are honest';
- 66 per cent were confident the CMC would 'properly investigate' complaints.

At the practical level, there is ample evidence of success by Australian integrity commissions in secondary prevention – identifying and stopping misconduct – and bringing offenders to justice. Most agencies provide investigation reports at their websites. The older agencies now have a long record of successful investigations of diverse forms of misconduct by public officials, including ending the careers of many corrupt politicians and public servants and sending many to jail (Taylor, 2009). Commissions have also been credited with prompting changes to procedures in government departments to reduce opportunities for corruption and affect positive cultural change (Salusinszky, 2009).

Despite these achievements, commissions often have difficulty demonstrating effectiveness in primary prevention. This is reflected, for example, in New South Wales's public opinion surveys. On average, 78 per cent of respondents have agreed that the ICAC is successful in exposing at least 'some' corruption, compared to 52 per cent who have agreed it is successful in 'preventing' or 'reducing' corruption (ICAC NSW, 2006, p.28; 2010a, p. 21). Furthermore, in New South Wales, the 2009 survey found that 41 per cent of respondents thought corruption was a 'major problem' in government departments, while 35 per cent thought corruption was a major problem in local government (ICAC NSW, 2010a, p. 9). Complaints and allegations against public officials have also tended to remain at high levels. While this is said to reflect confidence in the system, it does not reflect well in terms of reducing misconduct. At the same time, complaints of classic corruption tend to be in the minority.

There can be very little doubt that integrity commissions are seen as an essential institution in Australia. One government after another has been obliged to adopt them, if only to silence critics. But the mixed results of the above summary impact assessment suggest there is room for improvement. For example, while many of these agencies have a

10.1057/9781137335098

range of advanced, or 'smart', strategies available to them – including inquisitorial powers, covert operations and witness protection – they usually have no adjudicative powers and are highly selective about which cases they investigate, referring the large bulk of matters to in-house processing. Surveys of complainants who experience the system show widespread disappointment with what seems like a highly tokenistic response (Prenzler et al., 2013). The Hong Kong ICAC, by contrast, refers only 'non-corruption' matters back to departments (2012, p. 31). In Northern Ireland, the Police Ombudsman attracts very high levels of support from the public, complainants and police as a result of its independent processing of all complaints (Prenzler et al., 2013).

The big gun: a universal model?

Overall, within Grabosky and Braithwaite's spectrum, the Australian ACAs fall somewhere between 'benign big guns' and 'modest enforcers'. Many of the issues and experiences outlined above prompted Prenzler and Faulkner (2010) to summarize the main features of a model big gun integrity commission as follows (p. 259):

1 Conduct own-motion investigations;
2 Require attendance and answers to questions;
3 Hold public hearings;
4 Apply for warrants to search properties and seize evidence;
5 Engage in covert tactics – including listening devices, optical surveillance, undercover agents and targeted integrity tests;
6 Directly investigate the most serious and intermediate matters;
7 Make disciplinary decisions and manage a mediation programme;
8 Conduct research and risk reviews aimed at improving procedures and preventing misconduct;
9 Engage in public sector ethics training;
10 Prosecute complainants who are patently vexatious;
11 Account for its work using a variety of performance measures, including stakeholder satisfaction, prosecution outcomes and case study reports.

Powerful integrity commissions must also be held accountable to citizens. Consequently, oversight by a cross-party parliamentary committee provides a vital mechanism for scrutiny. Commissions should also develop a regional 'shop front' presence to provide public access. The Hong Kong ICAC has been described as 'the universal model' because of its 'resounding success in fighting corruption' (Heilbrunn, 2004, p. 3; see also OECD, 2013). But this view is tempered by recognition that other anti-corruption commissions have 'compiled a dismal record of effectiveness' (p. 2). There is also an argument that some jurisdictions have robust institutions which obviate the need for an omnibus agency. The majority of the countries in the top ten of the TI Perceptions index do not have anti-corruption commissions but have corruption levels that appear to be 'negligible' (Transparency International, 2001, p. 38). Different reasons for success apply in each case, but adequate legislation and judicial independence appear to be common ingredients, along with a multi-agency system that includes an auditor general and public service commission and/or an ombudsman (Heilbrunn, 2004; Transparency International, 2001; U4, 2010; UNODC, 2004).

It is also clear from the examples in this chapter that a properly designed commission can make a significant contribution to combating corruption and should constitute a worthwhile financial investment. At a minimum, the United Nations Convention against Corruption requires the establishment of a 'preventive anti-corruption body or bodies' and 'specialised authorities' (UNODC, 2004, pp. 10 & 16). Commissions provide a clear focus for corruption issues, a centre for co-ordinating other agencies with a role in combating corruption, and they can provide an assurance against allegations and rumours of corruption through provision of a fall-back mechanism for investigations.

This chapter has canvassed the applicability of situational crime prevention and regulatory theory to the task of designing effective corruption prevention systems. There is significant potential to close off or minimize corruption opportunities through a range of situational techniques. Extending guardianship appears to be a particularly fruitful line of development, including through a big gun anti-corruption commission. The big gun may not be essential in jurisdictions with stable low levels of corruption, but it appears to have been a crucial weapon in turning around the war on corruption in many jurisdictions. In some places though, ACAs may be more part of the problem than part of the solution.

There are important lessons for corruption prevention that must be borne in mind. Making it more of an effort to commit a corrupt act often involves increasing the amount of compliance required. Increasing compliance often irritates staff, slows down the work rate, and reduces productivity. Corruption prevention efforts often fail because the extra hurdles introduced are not necessarily proportional to the risk. Nobody wants to fill out pages of paperwork to acquire a low-value item, especially if the risk in acquiring it corruptly is very small. The key to corruption prevention is to increase, and not decrease productivity.

10.1057/9781137335098

Part III
Combating and Reducing Corruption

▶

10.1057/9781137335098

6
Preventing Corruption in Criminal Justice

Abstract: *This is the first of four chapters that examine ways to prevent corruption in specific settings. Criminal justice provides a good starting point because of the long history of varied and destructive forms of abuse of due process rights and responsibilities in this sector. Corruption has, and still does occur in the judiciary, as well as police and corrective services, in many locations. Examples are provided of how situational prevention principles can be used to eliminate or minimize corruption opportunities. These include the electronic recording of interviews with suspects, video surveillance of police actions, limits on pre-charge detention and entry/exit controls for prison custodial staff.*

Graycar, Adam and Prenzler, Tim. *Understanding and Preventing Corruption*. Basingstoke: Palgrave Macmillan, 2013. DOI: 10.1057/9781137335098.

Criminal justice systems in many countries have long histories of diverse and acute forms of corruption. Untold millions of people have suffered as a result of abuse of the justice system. The effects include wrongful conviction and false imprisonment, the execution of innocent persons, and the acquittal of guilty persons. Corruption amongst police and other justice officials facilitates crime and leads to neglect of the victims of crime. Members of the public have nowhere to turn for protection or to pursue justice unless they can afford private security.

Corruption in criminal justice has often involved perverting the course of justice for personal gain, such as graft or career benefits, or as a result of personal or ideological prejudices. The system is also vulnerable to forms of more generalized misconduct and unprofessional behaviour, including excessive force and assaults, inaction and neglect, and incompetence and laziness. The two problems of classic corruption and misconduct often occur in tandem, with corruption sometimes more difficult to identify.

To prevent corruption in this area, and other associated forms of misconduct, a complex set of overlapping laws, institutions and strategies is required. This chapter briefly reviews the nature and causes of corruption in criminal justice and describes an array of best-practice anti-corruption mechanisms. It then focuses on two key modern innovations: closing off opportunities for corruption by the application of recording technology in police interviews, and the establishment of a set of big gun regulatory agencies to serve as guardians against corruption and as a means for redressing miscarriages of justice.

Corruption in criminal justice systems

Criminal justice systems include three key institutions: police, criminal courts and corrections, along with allied organizations including public prosecutors, private and public legal defenders, and many other groups. The three main agencies are intended to work independently of each other. Police act in part as a feeder agency to the courts, and the courts act in part as a feeder agency to corrective services. This institutional separation of powers is designed to stop corruption and undue influence by preventing a monopoly in decision making. Nonetheless, criminal justice systems are extremely vulnerable to a wide range of forms of misconduct and abuse, including excessive force and brutality by police

10.1057/9781137335098

and prison officers; inaction, neglect of duty, bias, discrimination and politicization at all levels; as well as various forms of corruption such as graft, extortion and evidence tampering (Prenzler, 2009a).

It is not difficult to understand the causes of corruption in criminal justice. There is a great deal at stake in its operations. Victims of crime want offenders brought to justice. Offenders want to escape arrest and punishment. This creates demand-led corruption, where parties are willing to pay cash or other benefits to have 'justice' skewed in their favour. On the supply side, insiders are tempted to exploit their position by demanding payments for service – whether the service involves doing their job or not doing their job.

Variation in corruption in criminal justice is closely related to opportunity, which can be mapped across the TASP categories – Types, Activities, Sectors and Places. For instance, traditional police corruption was highly organized and involved long-standing systems of payoffs for the protection of illegal activities, including gambling, alcohol consumption, prostitution, abortion and drug trafficking (Prenzler, 2009a). This type of corruption has occurred in many countries since the development of investigations as a specialist police function in the nineteenth century, although it was often concentrated in vice squads operating in entertainment precincts. Patrol officers would avail themselves of more opportunistic forms of corruption, such as theft from a crime scene or payoffs from motorists to ignore a traffic violation. High levels of frontline discretion and low supervision were key factors in the pervasiveness of many types of police corruption.

Traditional open court systems provided some protection against more blatant forms of judicial corruption, but judges, prosecutors and court officials have been bribed by overt and covert means to speed up or slow down processes and obtain favourable outcomes. Correctional officers are faced with numerous opportunities to provide favours to prisoners or assist with early-release decisions. It is likely that for much of their longer-term histories, criminal justice systems were deeply corrupt – subject to all forms of nepotism, cronyism, graft and political manipulation (Critchley, 2007). 'Justice for sale' was probably much more an appropriate slogan than 'justice is blind'.

Traditions of corruption in criminal justice persist in many countries. For example, Jauregui (2007) spent a year observing and interviewing police in Uttar Pradesh, India. She found that every aspect of policing was corrupted by payments from both victims of crime and suspects.

10.1057/9781137335098

Fabrication or destruction of evidence to mislead the courts was standard practice. Internal police promotion processes were also organized by graft. In the UK, the recent Leveson Inquiry exposed a system in which police sold information to tabloid newspapers and engaged in inappropriate associations with the media, including through receipt of gifts and hospitality. Chapter 1 described the recent 'kids for cash' scandal in Pennsylvania, USA, involving payments to judges for sentencing juveniles to imprisonment in a private correctional facility.

Measurement

Measuring corruption in criminal justice is characterized by the same general problems of measuring corruption that we have already seen. Again, however, repeated measures from a variety of sources can provide a useful picture of trends and dimensions. Indicators include complaints and allegations, intelligence, convictions and disciplinary action, appeal and review outcomes, and public and stakeholder surveys and interviews. In combination, these can provide a fairly reliable picture of types and levels of corruption in the system. However, it would be fair to say that most justice departments do not engage in sufficient research on the topic, especially in terms of proactive audits to detect and measure possible corruption (Prenzler, 2009a).

As we have seen in this book, Transparency International is a major source of information on corruption (Chapter 3). The annual survey used in the Global Corruption Barometer asks respondents to identify institutions they believe are 'corrupt or extremely corrupt' (Transparency International, 2011). For 2010/11, out of 11 institutions across approximately 100 countries, overall, police were rated third worst at 55 per cent (behind political parties at 63 per cent and parliaments at 57 per cent). The judiciary was rated seventh at 46 per cent. There was, however, enormous variation across countries. For the judiciary, there were lows of 3 per cent in Denmark and 7 per cent in Norway, and for police, 5 per cent in Finland and 8 per cent in Denmark and Norway. The highest ratings for the judiciary were in Burundi at 91 per cent and Bolivia at 83 per cent, and for the police at 92 per cent in Burundi, Nigeria and Uganda.

The Global Corruption Barometer also asks survey respondents whether they paid a bribe to persons they came into contact with in different institutions in the last year. In the 2010/11 survey, 29 per cent

10.1057/9781137335098

of persons who had contact with police said they paid a bribe. This was the highest category, followed by the judiciary and customs at 23 per cent. (Corrections was not included.) Again, there was enormous variation between countries. For example, there were lows for the judiciary between 1 per cent in Denmark and Finland and for police, 0 per cent in Denmark and 1 per cent in Finland. The worst scores for the judiciary were 80 per cent in Cambodia and 78 per cent in Liberia, and for the police, 86 per cent in Liberia and 84 per cent in Bangladesh (Transparency International, 2011).

TI's annual *Global Corruption* reports are themed issues. The 2007 edition was concerned with judicial corruption, and drew on a variety of sources, including the regular perceptions and experience surveys. In 2006, in 33 of 62 countries, 50 per cent or more of respondents considered their 'judiciary/legal system' to be 'corrupt or very corrupt' (2007, p. 13). Of those who had contact with the judiciary in the past year, 12 per cent said they had paid a bribe (p. 12). The results in Africa were the highest at 21 per cent, and the European Union and other 'Western European countries' were the lowest at 1 per cent.

The TI (2007) report also provided in-depth investigative reports on different countries, focusing on specific problems and issues. Here are a few examples:

▸ In Mexico, 'the traffickers' judges' worked for drug barons by dismissing charges or reducing prison sentences to fines – which were easily paid by the traffickers.
▸ In Zimbabwe, the government of Robert Mugabe threatened independently minded judges, forcing them to resign, and replacing them with appointees who would implement the government's illegal land acquisition programme.
▸ In the USA, the system of electing judges led to conflicts of interest when campaign donors came before the courts.
▸ In Russia, surveys indicated graft was routine in many Russian courts, especially in lower courts away from the capital, with one study assessing the average price of 'obtaining justice' at $US358.

Miscarriages of justice

One of the most prominent effects of corruption in the sector is miscarriages of justice. The primary type of miscarriage of justice is the wrongful conviction and punishment of an innocent person. Miscarriages of justice also include the failure to prosecute offenders or their acquittal, as well as inappropriately harsh or lenient sentences, and excessive delays. The execution of an innocent person is arguably the ultimate miscarriage of justice.

As noted above, corruption is often associated with wider forms of misconduct, and miscarriages of justice involve corruption in the generalized sense of a perversion of justice, whatever the precise motive or cause. With execution in mind as arguably the worst outcome of corruption, it is instructive to consider the potential effect of injustices in death-penalty jurisdictions. The United States Death Penalty Information Center provides one perspective on this. The advent of DNA evidence since the late 1980s has been an extremely important tool in assisting exonerations. Research by the Center shows that, between 1973, when executions were resumed, and 2012, 140 people on death row were exonerated and freed (DPIC, 2013). A clear implication of this is that it is likely that many innocent people were executed in the past and that others are possibly still executed today. These high-profile death-penalty cases are also likely to represent the tip of the iceberg of fraud and error further down the scale of criminal court cases where DNA testing is not an option (Garrett, 2011).

Some of the most notorious miscarriages of justice occurred in England in the 1970s. They took place in the context of the mainland terrorist bombing campaign by the Provisional Irish Republican Army (IRA), and most of the victims of wrongful convictions were Irish. The cases involved extensive corruption by police, but not in the domain of traditional graft. The coerced and fabricated confessions and violations of due process entailed career benefits to police in closing the high-profile cases. Officers were under intense political pressure to achieve speedy arrests and convictions. Corruption involving the judges, lawyers and scientists was less clear-cut, although it was clear that across the professions there were misrepresentations of evidence and gross derelictions of duty.

The English cases are particularly important because they occurred in a judicial system that was touted as one of the fairest in the world and a model system for developing democracies. They drew international attention and led to major procedural reforms. The four main cases are summarized briefly below in a form that highlights key irregularities, system failures and impacts (Prenzler, 2009a; Rozenberg, 1992).

The *Guildford Four* case involved four young people sentenced to life imprisonment in 1975 for multiple murders associated with the 1974 Guildford Pub bombing. Two were also convicted over a second bombing. The main evidence in court was a set of inconsistent uncorroborated confessions signed under torture in police custody. The four were released in 1989 – after 14 years imprisonment – following a mass campaign and revelations that exculpatory evidence had been suppressed by police and the prosecution.

The *Maguire Seven* were imprisoned for lengthy periods over charges associated with an alleged suburban kitchen bomb factory. The convicted persons included a 14-year-old boy and an older man, Guiseppe Conlon, who died in prison. The case was notable for completely false evidence given by government scientists in relation to alleged incriminating traces of explosives.

The *Birmingham Six* were given life sentences in 1975 over the deaths of 21 people in two pub bombings in Birmingham. The men were convicted on the basis of alleged confessions, and testimony that two of them had handled explosives. The six were released in 1991 after 16 years in prison. In the final appeal, evidence was presented that the alleged traces of explosives in this and the Maguire Seven cases could have been acquired by a number of means including contamination in a forensic laboratory.

The other very high-profile case was that of *Judith Ward*, convicted over three IRA bombings. The obvious misconduct by senior scientists in similar cases led to a review of her case. Apart from the faulty forensic evidence, it was revealed that the prosecution hid evidence of Ward's mental illness and obvious lack of means to carry out the attacks, and had heavily edited a false confession. She was released from prison in 1992 after serving 18 years.

Opportunity factors

There is now a very well-established literature on miscarriages of justice that covers a spectrum of causal factors including error, incompetence, corruption and system inadequacies (e.g., HMSO UK, 1993; Roman et al., 2012; Rozenberg, 1992; Transparency International, 2007). These factors can add up to a long list. But within the list are a number of key opportunity factors amenable to situational interventions – addressed in the next section of this chapter. Examples of factors facilitating perversions of justice (Prenzler, 2009a, pp. 110–112) are:

- Excessive faith in... the self-regulatory capabilities of the system... includes unjustified faith in police probity. The naïve view that police will not lie in the witness box can carry through from the judiciary to jury prejudices that favour police testimony.

- Once a convicted person is locked away it is easy to ignore them and to repress any doubts about the validity of their conviction... Convicted persons, especially if they are in prison, usually have little or no access to the necessary resources to have a case reopened. The bar is also usually set very high for any review of a case. The defendant must produce fresh evidence or demonstrate errors by the prosecution or errors in the interpretation of law, or gross incompetence by the defence. Appeal courts are often considered to be reluctant to find fault with their colleagues, and a traditional system has limited institutional capacity for launching a fresh investigation funded by the state.

- The capacity for police to hold people without charge is also a major factor. People's defences quickly breakdown when they are isolated in a cell, denied food and sleep, and subjected to constant badgering by police. In their desperation to escape these conditions they will sign false confessions. The torture is hidden from the courts, where lawyers and judges fail to properly enquire into the sources of confessions. With the English cases, the new *Prevention of Terrorism Act* allowed police to hold suspects without charge for 48 hours, with a five day extension permitted by the Home Secretary. This allowed ample time for the victims to collapse under torture and sign false confessions...

- Another factor is perjury by police informants. Again, this involves excessive trust in the integrity of police who manage the informants. 'Jail house snitches' who claim a cellmate confessed to them feature prominently in miscarriage of justice cases...

- Sloppy forensics and an excessive faith in science and scientific witnesses has been another feature of miscarriages of justice cases.

10.1057/9781137335098

Opportunity reduction

The past 50 years have seen enormous numbers of scandals and problems associated with corruption in criminal justice in many countries around the world. This has led to the introduction of diverse reforms, including a professionalization agenda targeted at practitioners – emphasizing improved education, including in ethics, as well as appointment by merit, de-politicization, and innovations such as 'ethical interviewing'.

Other measures include clearer rules about evidence, jury selection and courtroom tactics. There has been a positive trend towards downgrading eyewitness and confessional evidence (Garrett, 2011). Courts are now expected to ensure confessions are voluntary and genuine, subject to reliability tests and corroboration. Eyewitness testimony should be subject to pre-trial tests with strict controls on police line-ups and photo arrays to protect against bias. There should also be in-trial instructions about problems in eyewitness identifications.

Other protective measures include sentencing guidelines for judges, disclosure requirements for both prosecution and defence, and access to legal aid for defendants. These measures are all necessary, but they can founder when opportunities for corruption and pressures on the job become irresistible. A rational choice or situational analysis of opportunity factors for corruption in criminal justice should lead to the development of possible preventive interventions that close off or minimize opportunities.

Opportunity reduction is an approach that should apply across the spectrum of corruption in the police, courts and corrections. For example, the sale of confidential information and unauthorized access to information has been a traditional area of police graft, fostered by easy access to targets. The initial roll-out of computer systems in policing greatly enlarged the opportunities for illicit access. However, improvements in security soon followed in response to the burgeoning problem. An IT security policy is now essential to any police integrity management system (e.g., CLEDS VIC, 2007). Access must be password controlled and limited by 'need to know' criteria. Access protocols must include a requirement that officers record the reasons for enquiries. All access should be tracked and audited. An alert should be activated when unauthorized access is attempted. Highly sensitive data must be kept on sequestered databases. From a situational point of view, these measures increase the effort and the risks for would-be offenders. Setting rules around access is supported by reducing or eliminating anonymity, entry/ exit controls, and strengthening of formal surveillance.

There are numerous other examples of opportunity-reducing measures in police corruption. Strict rules have been introduced in many jurisdictions for the management of informants. These include documenting the identity of informants, requiring senior officers to authorize relationships and make direct contact with informants, regular assessments of the informant's value, approvals for meetings, and the recording of all meetings and payments. When persons with criminal histories serve as witnesses there should be full disclosure of prior testimony and all deals with prosecutors (Garrett, 2011).

The high-risk area of police pre-charge detention has also been subject to stricter controls, including judicial approval for extensions, access to lawyers, communication with relatives and monitoring procedures. A limit of 24 to 48 hours has emerged as a guide for striking an appropriate balance between preventing abuses in detention and allowing police to conclude follow-up enquiries before filing charges (HMSO UK, 1993, pp. 29–30; Russell, 2007).

Another example concerns proactive post-conviction DNA testing, which has considerable potential to serve as an important counter to wrongful convictions. In this approach, authorities do not wait for petitions from aggrieved persons and their supporters but automatically re-test stored biological samples for accuracy of matches (Roman et al., 2012). The chance of forensic errors being identified through routine post-conviction testing will, in theory, further increase the risks and reduce the rewards of corrupt investigative processes. Of course, putting an end to the death penalty also opens the opportunity for redress that otherwise is permanently closed.

A further example concerns the traditional trade in contraband between prisoners and prison officers. In *Situational Prison Control*, Wortley (2002) describes how entry/exit controls need to be applied to staff as well as prisoners and visitors. External lockers for staff and clear plastic bags for staff possessions taken into prison assist in enlarging surveillance and controlling tools. Drug testing of prisoners and frequent searches of prisons, including with sniffer dogs, also assist at the demand end by denying benefits and disrupting markets.

The introduction of electronic recording of police interviews is a particularly successful example of situational corruption prevention. In England and Wales, the requirement for recording was introduced in the Police and Criminal Evidence Act 1984 (PACE). Development of the Act was influenced by the English miscarriages of justice cases while the victims were still fighting for justice. The 1993 report of the Runciman Royal Commission on Criminal Justice reviewed methods to prevent a repetition of these events. The Commission concluded that recording interviews was 'a strikingly successful innovation' in protecting suspects and police from false allegations (1993, p. 26).

The Commission's view is supported by impact research on this topic. In New South Wales, Dixon (2006) interviewed judges, prosecutors, defence lawyers and police, and analysed the content of tapes. Dixon found that recording was not foolproof in preventing the manipulation of suspects. However, he concluded, it was 'successful in putting an end to the long dispute about verballing [fabricating confessions], and is perceived by many criminal justice professionals to have increased guilty pleas, reduced trial length, reduced challenges to the admission of confessional evidence and increased public confidence in the justice process' (p. 330). Other research also shows widespread support from diverse practitioners (Garrett, 2011; Kassin et al., 2007).

The idea of audio and visual recording of police actions has been extended to a wide range of policing situations. Hand-held video cameras and mobile phone cameras have allowed for much greater citizenship participation in the police accountability process, including through uploading footage to the internet (Toch, 2012). Within policing, CCTV has been introduced into high-risk areas for abuse, such as watchhouses. Officers also often carry their own recorders to protect against false accusations. The past few years have seen considerable innovation in body-worn video and vehicle-mounted cameras. There is little systematic evidence on their impact but some pilot research indicates improvements in the quality of evidence and greater protection for police from false allegations. Covert video has been crucial to the gathering of evidence in undercover stings or 'integrity tests' against suspected highly secretive police corruption, especially in the lucrative drug trade (Prenzler, 2009a, ch. 4).

Guardianship and regulation

The English miscarriages of justice cases and similar cases in other countries have led to the introduction of much tighter regulation of criminal

10.1057/9781137335098

justice agencies, including through new regulatory bodies. In Australia, the introduction of both specialist and generalist anti-corruption commissions has been important to ending entrenched organized corruption rackets in policing, and exposing and stopping numerous smaller rackets in corrections (Prenzler, 2011). The Hong Kong ICAC is also noted for ending organized police corruption. Independent anti-corruption agencies extend guardianship and surveillance, and provide a safe haven for whistleblowers and witnesses.

Innovation has also occurred with a number of smaller big-gun-type regulatory agencies. For example, forensic laboratories are now expected to be independent of law enforcement and subject to quality-control standards and inspections by an independent accrediting agency (Garrett, 2011). Stricter standards have also been introduced for the preservation of crime scenes and handling of evidence. Forensic scientists are now normally subject to a code of conduct that requires them to act independently and report honestly on their findings, including where the evidence assists the defence. Defence observations of forensic tests, and access to independent re-testing, have also been important in improving surveillance and denying the benefits of fraud.

Miscarriages of justice and wider concerns about unethical conduct by lawyers have influenced a trend away from traditional self-regulation of the profession to greater external regulation (Ross, 2005). A number of jurisdictions now have legal service commissions or ombudsmen. These agencies normally have independence written into their governing legislation to guard against concerns about direct government control of a profession that is essential to the protection of civil liberties, including protection from government authorities. The main role of these agencies is to investigate complaints and prosecute misconduct through a range of sanctions, with an 'own motion' power to investigate matters without a complaint (Prenzler, 2009a). In doing this they provide public assurance and back-up to traditional licensing by professional associations.

Even the best criminal court appeals systems are limited by the absence of a properly resourced and independent agency to reinvestigate questionable cases. In light of this, the establishment of a permanent independent review commission was a major recommendation of the Runciman Commission, and such a body is widely considered as an important innovation in combating corruption and error in criminal justice. In the wake of Runciman, the UK Criminal Cases Review Commission (CCRC) was established in 1997; in 2012 it had a staff of 90.

10.1057/9781137335098

It has the capacity to engage in standard detective work re-investigating cases, including through fieldwork and forensic testing.

There has been considerable debate about the CCRC's effectiveness. It deals with an enormous workload and there is extremely high attrition of cases. It received 15,710 applications between 1997 and 2012; and out of the reviews completed in that period 3.4 per cent were referred to a court of appeal. Of these, 64 per cent resulted in a conviction being quashed. This might appear a meagre outcome, and it has been argued that the figure in fact overstates the Commission's achievements by including changes to sentences and re-convictions for less serious offences (cases downgraded from murder to manslaughter, for instance, as reported in the *Guardian* of 30 November 2012).

But there is a wider view that the Commission's presence and processes add to the legitimacy of the justice system and remedy at least some cases where the conviction was unsafe. One academic study concluded that:

> Not only is [the CCRC] an independent body, separate from both the executive and the judiciary, but it has enhanced resources, staffing and even, arguably, expertise. Most important, its receptive approach and attitude are in complete contrast to the reluctance, endemic in the governmental departments, to rein-vestigate cases with thoroughness. (Walker & McCartney, 2008 p. 197)

Most experts support the work of such agencies in helping to remedy and deter error, fraud and corruption. At the same time, they argue that to be effective review commissions should not be restricted by the need to identify 'fresh evidence' or abuses or errors in the court process. They also need to be able to address issues of 'factual truthfulness' and 'factual innocence' and be more flexible in prioritizing high-profile cases with a strong public-interest element (Naughton, 2012, pp. 210 & 223).

The criminal justice system is a high-risk domain for corruption and misconduct. In many jurisdictions there are insufficient safeguards to prevent or remedy resulting miscarriages of justice and loss of public confidence in the system. Many of these jurisdictions are in autocracies or developing democracies. But there are also recurring cases of corruption in many established democracies. Over time, numerous mechanisms have been developed that are designed to pre-empt corruption, and considerable improvement is evident in many places in the area of prevention. At the same time, closer attention to situational prevention principles and enhanced regulatory systems shows a great deal of potential and requires greater investment and development.

10.1057/9781137335098

7
Preventing Corruption in Public Sector Procurement

Abstract: *Government purchasing is an area where situational prevention measures can be used to combat the haemorrhage of taxpayer funds for private benefit. Analyses of these types of cases have highlighted the value of breaking down the procurement process into distinct phases and identifying opportunities for graft at each point. The introduction of rules about open competition and transparency can severely limit opportunities for collusion, along with a prohibition on gifts and benefits to procurement officers. An early intervention approach, through the use of warning flags, can prevent the development or completion of corruption conspiracies.*

Graycar, Adam and Prenzler, Tim. *Understanding and Preventing Corruption.* Basingstoke: Palgrave Macmillan, 2013. DOI: 10.1057/9781137335098.

10.1057/9781137335098

Purchasing of goods and services is an area of government activity where corruption is often commonplace, with numerous cases of major abuses on the record. This chapter begins by outlining some of the losses estimated to occur in procurement corruption, along with descriptions of modi operandi and opportunity factors. The focus of the chapter is on key prevention measures, including the application of warning flags at different stages of the procurement process. Attention is also paid to recent innovations in the areas of 'integrity pacts', 'corruption vulnerability assessments' and e-procurement. Examples are also provided of the implementation of reforms in procurement processes in different locations.

Dimensions, impacts and cases

A major report by Transparency International (2006) on Curbing Corruption in Public Procurement claimed that 'few activities create greater temptations or offer more opportunities for corruption than public sector procurement' (p. 13). The report also noted that corruption in government purchasing in some countries often involves 10 to 25 per cent of the contract price, but can be as high as 50 per cent. Research by Ware et al. (2011) indicates that the cost of paying bribes is often added to the final cost of a contract, rather than being absorbed within the profit margin. Corruption in procurement therefore represents a potentially large drain on the public purse. Other adverse impacts include faulty and inadequate service provision, inflated maintenance and replacement costs, workplace injuries and deaths, environmental damage, reduced efficiency and innovation, damage to public trust in government, and curtailment of economic development (Transparency International, 2006).

The scale of procurement corruption is highly variable, but some cases that have been brought to light have involved large sums of money. The following provides a brief snapshot of three prominent cases in different jurisdictions internationally.

In 1995, the Secretary-General of the North Atlantic Treaty Organization (NATO), Willy Claes, resigned after he was implicated in a bribery scandal over a military contract undertaken when he was Minister of Economic Affairs in the Belgian government during the late 1980s. Claes and the former Defence Minister Guy Coeme were subsequently found guilty of corruption. Aviation companies Agusta

10.1057/9781137335098

SpA and Dassault had made donations of approximately US$3 million to the Socialist Party. These were judged to be bribes made in return for military contracts worth US$520 million (Prenzler, 2009a, p. 21).

In 2004, former top-level US Department of Defense acquisition officer Darleen Druyan was sentenced to nine months in prison for her role in a conspiracy with Boeing to inflate the leasing price of aircraft. Druyan was negotiating a US$26 billion deal for 100 tanker aircraft. This was well above the likely market rate, and it was estimated that the existing fleet could have been upgraded for $3.6 billion. Druyan's motivation was to secure a vice-presidency at Boeing, with a salary of $250,000 per annum. She also illegally passed information to Boeing on a rival bid and favoured Boeing in a number of other multi-million dollar negotiations. A former Boeing Chief Financial Officer, Michael M. Sears, was also jailed (Branstetter, 2005).

In 2008, the New South Wales Independent Commission against Corruption found that two project managers in the New South Wales Fire Department, Christian Sanhueza and Clive Taylor, had acted corruptly. The men submitted false tenders for capital works and maintenance to create the appearance of competition. Contracts worth approximately AU$6 million were awarded to front companies controlled by Sanhueza. The work was then delegated to subcontractors at lower prices. Managers signed off on Sanhueza's and Taylor's assessments of the bids and the work without proper scrutiny. The two men shared illicit profits of $2.4 million. They also received kickbacks in the form of televisions and computers for referring work to another company (ICAC NSW, 2008).

Grey areas

There are a number of practices in government spending that are susceptible to corruption but where rules to ensure integrity are frequently under-developed. Examples might not constitute 'procurement' as such, but they do involve government payments. These areas include grants and awards – often for welfare programmes, the arts and community clubs. Payments in these categories are vulnerable to undue influence, favouritism and 'pork barrelling' (local expenditures designed to attract votes rather than meet genuine needs on fair criteria), but they are often exempt from strict procurement protocols because they are not commercial transactions. Another common grey area concerns access to

10.1057/9781137335098

politicians or public officials by lobbyists seeking to promote the interests of clients (see Chapter 9, on town planning). These meetings might relate to potential government purchases (as well as decisions such as zoning) but occur outside specific tender processes.

Similarly, the status of gifts and benefits provided to managers and procurement officials by tender companies may be questionable (see also the section 'Gift Giving and Rent Seeking' in Chapter 2). These are often accepted as forms of customary hospitality and a standard means of facilitating business that provides harmless minor benefits, or 'perks', for government employees. However, it is increasingly recognized that gift-giving and hospitality create intrinsic conflicts of interest and are intended to impress a sense of obligation on the recipient.

In the state of Queensland, Australia, for example, newspapers carried out a series of investigative reports in the 1990s and 2000s on gifts provided to top decision makers in government procurement. The Director-General of the Public Works and Housing Department 'accepted free tickets to the Three Tenors concert from Telstra and was accused of later granting the telecommunications company an AU$200,000 contract' (Prenzler, 2009a, p. 22). It was also revealed that the Director of the Information Management Division of the Police Service received 82 gifts in five years – including free golf games, theatre tickets and tickets to sporting events – from companies seeking to do business with the police. None of the cases led to prosecutions.

Another grey area concerns excessive expenditures. Even if bribery is not involved, waste and excess are often seen as types of corruption involving misuse of taxpayers' funds, with specific beneficiaries amongst suppliers and public servants. In its special report on procurement, Transparency International included a number of examples of excessive expenditures from local government in Malaysia (2006, pp. 171–172). These included a contract between a council and a florist for the delivery of over 1,000 flowers per week for five years, and the purchase of 10 thoroughbred horses from overseas for an equestrian police squad to combat minor crime.

Modi operandi and opportunity

Procurement corruption is particularly difficult to both detect and prevent, in large part because 'Procedures are often complex. Transparency of the process is limited, and manipulation is hard to detect. Few people who become aware of corruption complain publicly, since it is not their own, but government money, which is being wasted' (Transparency International, 2006, p. 13).

Ware et al. (2011) analysed a variety of types of procurement corruption in different settings internationally and identified general factors that make public sector purchasing prone to corruption. As noted above, there are often large amounts of money involved. Specifically, Ware et al. observed that procurement is also vulnerable to fraud because 'In contrast with the other major components of a country's public expenditure, public procurement usually involves a relatively low volume of high-value transactions (typically a few hundred procurement transactions conducted annually by each public institution, the most valuable of which may involve millions of dollars)' (2011, pp. 65–66).

While this may be the case, procurement corruption can be attractive at much lower rates. Scams involving a high volume of low-value items can be highly lucrative, especially when perpetrated over several years. For example, in Australia, small-scale cases have involved purchasing officers in government departments receiving very small inducements (gift vouchers for, say, $50) to purchase supplies like photocopier toner from a particular supplier (CCC WA, 2011). The supplier in question was able to sell a lot of toner right across the country at inflated costs, and in quantities far in excess of that needed, but the nature of the purchases often slipped under the radar.

An additional risk factor is that public procurement often involves high levels of discretion by decision makers. Discretion can involve party-political dimensions, with politicians seeking electoral advantages through large expenditures – such as major road projects. The politicians may sit on selection committees or pressure public servants to make decisions that benefit the party rather than the public interest. Ware et al. also argued that the risk of corruption is higher in developing countries, 'where the legislative, regulatory and institutional frameworks put in place to curtail the discretionary aspects of public procurement tend to be weaker than those in the West' (2011, p. 66).

The situation in developing nations can be exacerbated by private sector companies' greater dependence on government for business. Opportunities for procurement corruption in developing and developed nations have been enlarged in recent decades by the trend towards privatization and outsourcing of government services (Transparency

10.1057/9781137335098

International, 2006). There are also many areas of procurement that are particularly vulnerable to corruption, including emergency procurement or specialist purchases, where normal controls are bypassed (Ware et al., 2011).

Types of procurement corruption and opportunity factors

Ware et al. (2011, p. 69ff) developed a typology of procurement corruption that included information about the modus operandi of offenders and the means by which opportunities are exploited. As we have seen in this book, identifying opportunity factors assists in the custom design of prevention strategies. The three main schemes the researchers identified are outlined as follows.

'Scheme 1: Kickback Brokers – Agents and Local Representatives' relates to the practice of bribing procurement officers through an intermediary. This may involve a foreign company employing a 'business development agent' at the local level who ostensibly acts as an intermediary on practical matters but whose primary task is to bribe politicians and local procurement officers.

'Scheme 2: Bid Rigging' describes an ostensibly fair and open tender system that is manipulated behind the scenes to favour one or more bidders over others. This can be done by collusion between an inner group of bidders who might agree to stagger contracts by taking turns at submitting low bids. In some cases, this might be done without the knowledge of procurement officials. In other cases, officials might facilitate the fraud by various means, including writing criteria into tenders favourable to selected bidders. Within this scheme, Ware et al. (2011, p. 73) describe five specific methods:

1 With 'bid suppression', competitive companies may be persuaded not to bid or withdraw bids – through offers of subcontracting, for example;
2 'Complementary bidding' involves parties to the scam submitting untenable bids to create the appearance of competition;
3 'Bid rotation' involves parties agreeing to take turns to present and win the best tender;
4 With 'customer or market allocation', insiders agree to keep to specific government clients or geographic areas and not compete

against each other – this may involve submitting dummy bids outside their territory;

5 'Low balling' involves the favoured company submitting a low bid to win the contract, after which the corrupt procurement officials assist the company to renegotiate the price on the basis of alleged unforeseen cost increases.

'Scheme 3: Use of Front or Shell Companies' often occurs in tandem with schemes 1 and 2. Because these companies barely exist as material entities, they can disappear with downpayments without the corrupt official being identified.

Preventing public sector procurement corruption

All procurement needs to occur within an institutional framework designed to minimize corruption. Chapters 4 and 5 of the book set out the key elements of this framework, including international agreements and laws. Situational crime prevention techniques and regulatory theory will further assist in the design, testing and refinement of strategies. Rule setting, for example, is an essential first step to ensure laws against procurement corruption are clearly articulated without ambiguities hindering the prosecution process or providing excuses for misconduct. Independent complaints investigation is also essential; along with independent financial auditing, and compulsory whistleblower legislation and whistleblower protections.

The following provides more specific guidance on corruption prevention in procurement. Early-intervention approaches can be used to detect and shut down corruption schemes when they are in an embryonic stage. This type of secondary prevention can significantly reduce losses and contribute to recovery of most or all losses. Primary prevention is, of course, preferable in precluding the initiation of a conspiracy or plan by completely closing off opportunities. Front-end control mechanisms are likely to slow the bidding and approval process, and this can be difficult because of the need for governments to carry on business efficiently without undue delays.

Nonetheless, the costs of procurement corruption provide a ready justification for investment in pre-emptive strategies. Some elements of prevention, such as appropriate rule setting and procedural changes, require very little expense. Additional measures can be developed within a situational prevention framework. High-profile prosecutions discourage imitation. Recovery of proceeds of crime denies benefits. From the point of view of both situational prevention and regulatory theory, guardianship, formal surveillance and deterrence can be significantly enhanced through the work of a big gun anti-corruption commission. Other strategies of relevance include assisting compliance, reducing anonymity and entry/exit screening.

From a primary prevention perspective, the 'grey areas' outlined above require attention in many jurisdictions. In some cases, it is simply a matter of eliminating ambiguity by setting rules to prohibit actions such as offering or accepting gifts or benefits. Other examples include mandatory public disclosures of political donations, registers of all meetings with lobbyists, declarations of conflicts of interest, and the exclusion of persons with conflicts of interest from decision-making roles or influence. Failure to declare conflicts of interests should be grounds for disciplinary action or employment termination. Areas of procurement that are permitted to occur outside standard open competitive procedures – such as small expenditures and emergency expenditures – require strict controls such as a hierarchy of approvals and close post hoc performance evaluation. Bidders need to be informed of these rules, both to deter attempts at corruption and to facilitate compliance. Stakeholder input through responsive regulation can also assist in preventing wasteful and excessive expenditures.

Examples of primary corruption prevention strategies in procurement that should be in place pre-contract include the following (Transparency International, 2006, p. 35ff):

▶ mandatory needs assessments, with a requirement for written justifications, and opportunities for consultation with, and objections from, stakeholders;
▶ transparency through full public disclosure of tender terms, tenders, outcomes and reasons for outcomes;
▶ banning previous offenders;
▶ requiring disclosure of previous convictions or investigations;
▶ strict protocols or bans on contact between companies and procurement officers;
▶ clear criteria for quality as well as price;
▶ decisions should be made by a group not an individual;

▸ time limits on positions and staff rotation in procurement offices to prevent the development of personal relationships.

Yellow and red warning flags

Ware et al. (2011) describe the use of both 'yellow flags' (matters of concern) and 'red flags' (warnings of a very serious problem) in relation to secondary and primary prevention. They apply the concept of yellow flags to four major phases in procurement. These warning flags should trigger investigations or other actions, such as the exclusion of bids, which will shut down potential or embryonic scams. The four phases are (p. 81):

1   Project identification and design;
2   Advertising, prequalification, bid document preparation, and submission of bids;
3   Bid evaluation, post-qualification and award of contract; and,
4   Contract performance, administration and supervision.

Examples of yellow flags at each phase include the following:

1   Project specification and selection processes are vague; cost estimates do not reflect common market rates;
2   Advertising is minimal; timeframes for bids are overly restrictive;
3   Bids are not open to public scrutiny; some bidders have obstacles placed in their path (such as altered tender submission locations); tenders are accepted after the closing date;
4   Monitoring criteria are different to those specified in the original tender criteria; the evaluation committee lacks expertise; modifications are accepted which benefit the contractor.

In addition, Ware et al. apply the concept of red flags to the three procurement corruption schemes described above (kickback brokers, bid rigging and shell companies). In the case of schemes involving kickback brokers, they list the following warning signs (pp. 71–72; see alsoTransparency International, 2006, p. 34ff):

▸ Improper bidder selection, for example, repeated contract awards by sole sourcing of a single supplier without competition.
▸ Involvement of an unnecessary middleman or local agent.

- ▸ Procurement officials who accept inappropriate gratuities.
- ▸ Unexplained or conspicuous wealth of government officials.
- ▸ Certain government officials having a widely known reputation in the local community for demanding or accepting bribes.
- ▸ Under-delivery or poor performance of a public contract by a favoured contractor, followed by recurrent contract awards.
- ▸ Former government officials acting as suppliers or as a local agent.
- ▸ Close personal relationship, including family ties, between suppliers or local agents and government officials.

The following include examples of red flags relevant to bid rigging scams (pp. 74–75):

- ▸ Identical bids submitted by different bidders either with respect to individual line items in the bids, or to the total bid prices.
- ▸ All bids submitted are substantially higher than the procuring entity's cost estimate.
- ▸ The range of bid prices shows a wide gap between the winner and all other bidders.
- ▸ Qualified bidders do not bid, especially if they initially took steps to bid.

Red flags relevant to shell companies include (p. 78):

- ▸ Previously unknown companies.
- ▸ A subcontractor company is registered in a secret jurisdiction.
- ▸ The subcontractor company lacks visible corporate facilities.

Innovations in prevention

This section briefly describes three areas of promising developments in procurement corruption prevention.

Integrity Pacts have been promoted as a key tool in the fight against procurement corruption (Transparency International, 2006, p. 117). An integrity pact is a signed agreement between parties in the public–private procurement process. By signing up to the agreement the parties make a commitment to fairness, transparency and accountability. The process of negotiating and signing a pact ensures standards are put in writing; and it obliges parties to become familiar with the basic requirements of open,

10.1057/9781137335098

ethical and legal procurement – including an explicit commitment not to solicit or accept bribes or engage in unfair practices, including offering and accepting gifts. Other provisions normally include community participation, independent monitoring and whistleblower protection.

Corruption Vulnerability Assessments (CVAs) are described by Ware et al. as 'the newest and most innovative idea in the field of fraud and corruption prevention' (2011, p. 105). This is a specific application of a common risk-assessment methodology that seeks to forecast all threats to the viability of a business or institution. Corruption has often been a neglected aspect of this process. Risk assessments are supported by matrixes that assign threat levels to crime or harm categories, based on the concepts of 'criticality' – the extent to which an event would adversely affect the functioning of the agency – and 'probability' – an assessment of the likelihood of an event occurring (Prenzler, 2009b). CVAs should include the following (Ware et al., 2011, pp. 105–106):

▸ 'Country and risk assessments' (sample questions are: is corruption common practice? are there strong or weak in-country anti-corruption systems?)
▸ 'System and control reviews' (e.g., are auditors trained in corruption risks?), and
▸ A 'human factors' review (e.g., what are the financial backgrounds and reputations of key individuals?)

This 'enhanced due diligence' needs to be continued into a monitoring phase once contracts have been signed and work progresses (p. 106).

Ware et al. state that e-procurement can improve efficiency in government business but it can also assist in preventing corruption. The internet allows tender requests to be widely advertised. The use of online submissions can ensure all information fields are completed and documents attached before submissions are accepted. Online bid submission reduces or eliminates the need for human contact, thereby reducing the opportunity for conspiracy. Email can also provide a record of all communications. Post-contract disclosures of bids can be conveniently listed at the department website. However, e-procurement is not invulnerable to corruption, nor is it an alternative to other forms of corruption prevention, but works best within a mix of strategies. In particular, government officials need to engage in due diligence to ensure online bidders are bona fide companies with a physical presence and resources to carry out work.

10.1057/9781137335098

Case studies

The 2006 Transparency International report Curbing Corruption in Public Procurement includes case studies on the implementation of positive strategies to stop corruption in government purchasing. The following two examples illustrate some of the potential achievements, as well as potential problems, in implementation.

The Malaysian private sector introduced a number of initiatives in the 2000s designed to combat corruption, with likely beneficial impacts on public sector procurement. The Stock Exchange introduced the Mandatory Accreditation Programme (MAP) and the Continuing Education Programme (CEP), which 'contributed to higher awareness of governance issues and the general raising of standards despite some concerns over implementation at times' (Transparency International, 2006, p. 155). In 2003, the Malaysian International Chamber of Commerce and Industry set up a Standing Committee for Improving Business Ethics, which was intended to educate and support members in areas of good governance and business ethics. At the federal government level, in 2004, the Prime Minister introduced an open tendering process for government work. Specifically, TI reported (2006, p. 157) that:

> Government procurement was improved concretely when the Prime Minister launched the GLC Transformation Manual in 2005 to improve the effectiveness of government-linked companies (GLC). This has been followed by the launching of a guide book, popularly known as the 'Red Book' (because of its red cover), to promote best practice in procurement processes and procedures for government-linked companies.
>
> According to the Prime Minister, the Red Book potentially will save 4 to 9 billion Malaysian Ringgit of the estimated 50 billion Malaysian Ringgits in procurement of the GLCs. This would be a saving of 8–18%.
>
> This drive for better delivery systems and better procurement systems is not happening in a vacuum. It is part of the Prime Minister's push for more transparency and integrity in his overall campaign to make Malaysia a first class or first world country with a first class mentality.

The second case occurred in the District of Solok, in West Sumatra in Indonesia. The district Regent was motivated to address the issue of procurement corruption after attending the 2003 International Anti-Corruption Conference held in Korea (Transparency International, 2006, p. 120ff). The integrity pact model was adopted following planning workshops, training in integrity pact principles and drafting of a localized version of a pact. The finalized pact was signed by relevant public officials and the Chief of the Public Works Unit. Key features included the periodic promulgation of information, an anti-bribery sticker campaign and promotion of a complaint system. The Regent recognized that an implementation plan was needed to ensure the pact was not simply a token document. Consequently, a Commission of Transparency and Participation was established, along with an Independent Monitoring Board and a Complaints Management Board.

TI conducted a qualitative assessment of the impact of reform one year after implementation of the integrity pact. The approach included a useful systematic checklist, with qualitative descriptors regarding implementation of each element of the pact. However, the sources for the assessment were not explained in detail. Apart from records of legislation and decrees, anecdotal reports from interested parties appear to have been the main source. TI concluded that (2006, pp. 125–126):

> Integrity Pacts…seem to be an effective way to reduce illegal payments. According to some, most bidders in Solok are now reluctant and even refuse to pay if they are asked for illegal payments. Previously, bidders were victims of constant extortion. Even though companies are the actors providing bribes, they often saw this as a necessity if they wanted to win a contract for a public project. It was also viewed as necessary for many contractors to bribe the project supervisor if they wanted a project report to be accepted, which was necessary for the disbursement of project funds.

These case studies are useful, but they are also indicative of a common problem of data deficits in planning and evaluating anti-corruption reforms. This is also symptomatic of a general problem with the literature in this field. A number of detailed guides and principles are now available (e.g., ICAC Hong Kong, 2013; ICAC NSW, 2013; Transparency International, 2006) – which are derived in large part from documented system failures. The recommended strategies in these guides appear to be necessary and are likely to be effective, especially when implemented as a full package. However, what is also needed are case studies of documented successes in large-scale and sustained reductions in procurement corruption. It is much easier to find examples of major frauds that have been discovered and stopped than evaluations of primary prevention initiatives using measures of corruption in a time series format. As we have seen with situational crime prevention, pre- and post-intervention data are essential to demonstrate what works. (The inclusion of a control

10.1057/9781137335098

group can also enhance the validity of findings, although this is not always feasible.) In the case of corruption, data do not necessarily have to be in the form of reported offences; they can include perception and experience surveys and/or other indicators of corruption (see Chapter 3 on measuring corruption).

The literature on integrity in public health systems includes some examples of attempts to evaluate the impact of tightened procurement rules. These examples are developed in more detail in the following chapter.

Procurement corruption has a long history in the public sector. Abuse of government purchasing has been responsible for significant losses to taxpayers and diminution in the integrity of government service delivery. Numerous other harms derive from this type of crime. There are many cases documented in the literature concerning large frauds and their modi operandi. A great deal is now known about the opportunity factors that have allowed these frauds to be perpetrated. From this experience a solid literature has emerged on best practice in detection and prevention, including numerous laws, procedures, strategies and institutions. It is likely that procurement corruption can be minimized through a robust regime of opportunity reduction that follows this best-practice template. However, quality research is needed that will more reliably demonstrate the effectiveness of these strategies in practice.

10.1057/9781137335098

8
Preventing Corruption in Public Health

Abstract: *Public health services can be exploited in the procurement of medical supplies, in influence peddling over prescription practices and drug testing, through poor service standards, and through over-billing and fraud. Understanding opportunity factors is, again, the key means to designing prevention systems and strategies. System vulnerabilities stem from excessive discretion, lack of scrutiny and transparency, and under-enforcement or non-enforcement of rules. The chapter reports on a number of intervention studies that provide promising examples of evaluated practice in corruption prevention in hospitals.*

Graycar, Adam and Prenzler, Tim. *Understanding and Preventing Corruption*. Basingstoke: Palgrave Macmillan, 2013. DOI: 10.1057/9781137335098.

10.1057/9781137335098

Corruption causes many different types of harm, for example, substandard infrastructure, urban blight, injustices including wrongful convictions, and loss of trust in public authorities, to name just a few. Corruption in public health is an area that is particularly insidious, with significant potential for injury, death and the denial of services essential for people's health and well-being. Victims are disproportionately likely to come from vulnerable or disadvantaged populations – including children, pregnant women and babies, the elderly, the disabled and the poor, but people from all walks of life can be affected.

People who enter the health professions do so ostensibly to serve others, so when these people behave corruptly, a disillusion factor, bordering on an insult, can also be added to the harmful effects of corruption in public health. Health professions should be both professionally and social motivated, and for them to perpetrate the harms associated with corruption is particularly egregious.

From a prevention point of view, we can also see that in public health a high-trust model of integrity management is unlikely to succeed. Corruption in health systems is heavily influenced by rational choices and opportunity factors. The design of prevention strategies therefore needs to remain cognizant of agents' perceptions of the likely risks and rewards entailed in corrupt practices. The approach to corruption prevention needs to be as systematic and thorough as possible in health as in any other sector. While anti-corruption measures should not unjustifiably impede the frontline delivery of medical services, there is a particularly compelling case for action given the high stakes entailed in failing to address corruption opportunities in the sector.

The nature and extent of corruption in public health

As we have seen in regard to other government sectors, types of corruption in public health are highly variable and levels of corruption are highly variable. For example, surveys conducted in Latin America by Di Tella and Savedoff (2001, p. 15) identified quite different types of abuses in the sector, including

> theft of medical supplies, absenteeism by doctors and nurses, illegal payments for services, excessive payments for inputs and contracted services, favouritism in appointments and promotions, unauthorised use of public facilities for private medical practice, unnecessary referrals to private consultations, and inducement of unnecessary medical interventions.

10.1057/9781137335098

The Transparency International Global Corruption Barometer provides valuable information about corruption, but the health sector is not included as a separate entity in these surveys. However, TI's 2006 Global Corruption Report was focused on health services and provides an international perspective on the issue with ongoing currency. The report concluded that, in the health sector:

> [c]orruption might mean the difference between life and death for those in need of urgent care. It is invariably the poor in society who are affected most by corruption because they often cannot afford bribes or private health cover. But corruption in the richest parts of the world also has its costs. Hundreds of millions of dollars are lost each year to insurance fraud and corruption in rich countries, including the United States and the United Kingdom. (Transparency International, 2006, p. vii; see also Brooks et al., 2012)

The report also found that corruption in health care 'severely hampered' the achievement of three of the United Nations' key 'millennium development goals' for 2005: 'reducing child mortality, improving maternal health and combating HIV/AIDS, malaria and other diseases' (p. xii).

One type of health sector corruption common in many countries and highlighted in the TI report was a 'corruption tax' on patients (Rose in Transparency International, 2006, p. 40). Persons appearing at hospitals and clinics, especially in underfunded public systems, are expected to pay cash for treatment meant to be free on a triage basis. This system of extortion means that many people receive either no medical attention or substandard treatment. The TI report included testimony from victims of this practice in Casablanca (2006, p. 74):

> My husband injured his hand at work and was taken to a public hospital. He had to pay 300 dirhams (US $33) to get an X-ray and 200 to have the injury stitched. He then had to pay another 500 dirhams just to be allowed to stay in the hospital.

> When my wife went to the hospital they examined her and prescribed some pills. They said that none were available there, but if we paid 20 or 30 dirhams (US $2–3), someone could provide the 'free medication'. The problem is, we can't afford the drugs.

The following provides examples of indicators cited in the TI report which reveal something of the potential scale of corruption problems in public health:

10.1057/9781137335098

▶ Surveys and other sources indicate that 'informal payments' (a corruption tax) accounted for up to 56 per cent of expenditures on health in the Russian Federation, 30 per cent in Poland and 80 per cent in Georgia (p. 64).

▶ A survey in Morocco found that four out of five respondents believed corruption in public health was 'common to very common', while 59 per cent of those requiring treatment in a hospital reported they had paid to be examined or admitted (p. 75).

▶ A survey in Central and Eastern Europe found that 'five out of six people who see nearly all their officials as corrupt think their health system is either very bad or not so good; and almost four-fifths who think a majority of officials are corrupt see the health service in negative terms' (p. 40).

▶ In the United States, with national expenditure on health put at over $1.6 trillion, most estimates of fraud against Medicare (a government-subsidized health insurance scheme for the elderly) and some Medicaid programmes (which provide means-tested health care for low-income earners) put losses in the range 5–10% (pp. 16, 19; see also Sparrow, 2000a).

▶ In Bogota, Columbia, conservative estimates suggested that corruptly inflated prices in hospital procurement involved losses of Col$3,025 billion, sufficient to fund health cover for an additional 24,000 persons (p. 51).

Corruption in pharmaceuticals is an area of particular concern. Payments to hospital administrators or doctors to induce them to purchase or prescribe particular drugs represent a major problem. Companies often avoid bribery charges by operating in the grey area of gifts and benefits, including paying for holidays and attendance at conferences in exotic and luxurious settings. The TI study on corruption in the health sector reported that in the United States pharmaceutical and related companies were spending approximately $16 billion each year on marketing products to doctors, including $2 billion on meals and events (Kassirer in Transparency International, 2006, pp. 85–91; see also Sparrow, 2000a). Some attempts by drug companies to obtain influence without detection can be inventive. For example, the Polish subsidiary of a US-based drug company made large donations to a foundation for restoring castles run by the director of a health authority which funded pharmaceutical purchases (Cohen in Transparency International, 2006, pp. 77–85).

10.1057/9781137335098

Private sector research grants and other forms of payments to scientists engaged in drug research represent another area of risk, as does 'capture' of drug regulators. In the USA in the 1990s, 'most of the top medical authorities...and virtually all of the top speakers on medical topics [were] employed in some capacity by one or more of the country's pharmaceutical companies' (Kassirer in Transparency International, 2006, p. 87). In the mid-2000s, the US Food and Drug Administration was hit by scandals over approvals for numerous drugs that were later withdrawn from the market (in Transparency International, 2006). The approvals were made in the context of close relationships between the regulator and drug companies, including regulator salaries funded by industry. (For other examples of unethical practices in the development and promotion of medicines see Elliott, 2010 and Goldacre, 2012).

Financial conflicts of interest have also muddied the water in medical litigation. Kassirer (in Transparency International, 2006) describes a US study which compared the readings of chest X-rays by two groups of radiographers. The groups were trained to the same standard but one group had been hired by law firms engaged in litigation against companies who allegedly exposed litigants to lung damage, while the other group were independent persons engaged for the purpose of the study. It was found that the so-called 'hired hands' assessed 96–97 per cent of X-ray films as abnormal, whereas the 'independents' assessed 6–7 per cent as abnormal.

Another example of corruption in the sector is the exploitation of donor funds for health care in developing countries, especially in the area of supply of affordable medicines. This is considered a major problem that significantly detracts from the impact of health programmes (Tayler & Dickinson in Transparency International, 2006, pp. 104–111). A closely related area of fraud and corruption concerns the manufacture and sale of fake or substandard drugs. Drug counterfeiting, 'facilitated by corruption, kills en masse' (Transparency International, 2006, p. xvi). For example, research in Nigeria found 'cases of water being substituted for life-saving adrenaline and of active ingredients being diluted by counterfeiters, triggering drug-resistant strains of malaria, tuberculosis and HIV, the world's biggest killers' (p. xvi). In one year alone in China it was estimated that approximately 192,000 people died from counterfeit drugs (Transparency International, 2006, p. 84).

10.1057/9781137335098

Latin American case studies

The challenge of understanding the extent of corruption in the health sector has been assisted in part by a set of innovative studies carried out in seven Latin American countries in the 1990s, collected by Di Tella and Savedoff (2001) and published by the Inter-American Development Bank.

The collection included findings from a survey in Costa Rica, which included doctors, nurses and patients. Respondents were asked to rate corruption in public institutions on a scale from 0, 'indicating no corruption', to 10, indicating 'the highest degree of corruption' (Di Tella & Savedoff, 2001, p. 201). Corruption in the Ministry of Health was given a rating of 5.4 by patients, 5.3 by doctors and 6.7 by nurses. In addition (p. 202):

▸ 79.5 per cent of doctors and 97.8 per cent of nurses saw corruption as a factor in 'physician absenteeism'.

▸ 85.4 per cent of doctors and 90.1 per cent of nurses indicated that patients were subject to unauthorized charges.

▸ 71.2 per cent of doctors and 82.9 per cent of nurses believed there was a problem with theft of supplies and equipment.

More developed work in the area is exemplified by a study in Bolivia. With the goal of 'getting a fix on corruption', Gray-Molina et al. (in Di Tella & Savedoff, 2001, p. 31) analysed price differentials for medical supplies across 30 hospitals. They also conducted perception and experience surveys with hospital administrators, doctors, nurses and patients. The price analysis revealed large differences across four basic medical items. For example, prices paid for normal saline varied between Bs 1.20 and Bs 18.50. Prices for ethyl alcohol varied between Bs 1.30 and Bs 8.00. It appeared that local overpricing might have provided a partial explanation, but corruption was the most likely factor in these large differences.

The survey research lent support to this view and enabled an enlarged perspective on the types and extent of corruption in the system. Respondents generally scored perceived corruption levels as much lower than other public institutions including the police, customs, the supreme court and the presidency. At the same time, a large proportion of respondents believed there was at least some corruption in public hospitals. The researchers used a scale from 'never' any corruption, through 'a little', 'some' and 'a lot' to 'always'. Between 17 per cent and

22 per cent of respondents thought there was at least 'a little' corruption, while 44 per cent of patients scored the system from 'some' to 'always'. The latter figure for doctors was 47 per cent and 27 per cent for nurses (Gray-Molina et al. in Di Tella & Savedoff, 2001, p. 40). Respondents' reported perceptions of levels of corruption increased when they were asked about specific types of corruption in public hospitals. For example (p. 41):

- ▶ 64 per cent of doctors and 74 per cent of nurses thought there was some or more theft of supplies.
- ▶ 80 per cent of doctors believed there was some or more corruption in 'scheduling procedures' (including 49 per cent who said 'always').
- ▶ 67 per cent of doctors believed there was some or more corruption in procurement of cleaning services.
- ▶ 55 per cent of doctors believed there was some or more corruption in procurement of medical supplies.

The research in Bolivia by Gray-Molina et al. (in Di Tella & Savedoff, 2001) included a survey subsample. This group was asked about illicit payments under 'the most important' government health grant programme, which provided care for infants and mothers (p. 31). The survey identified 281 'clients' of the programme. Forty per cent indicated they had made 'illegal payments' for services related, amongst other things, to 'hospitalisation, surgery, medication, material and supplies' (p. 44).

These studies show the value of multiple methods in assessing corruption levels and informing authorities on the need for action. The analysis of payment differentials, as one example, can be used to assess possible fraud and over-billing by doctors. Survey or interview data can add weight and detail to the findings on billing. Multiple data sources are also useful for diagnostics in designing anti-corruption interventions and targeting priority areas. Ongoing data collection also allows for impact assessments of the interventions.

Influences on corrupt practices

The introduction to this chapter cited the common view that health professionals should be unlikely to engage in corruption because of the humanitarian nature of their work. However, the evidence about the scale of corrupt practices in public health in different countries indicates strongly that personal and professional ethics are insufficient to prevent systemic abuses. Public health is an attractive, and often an easy, target for corruption because of the combination of large amounts of money, strong demand for services essential to human life and well-being, and poor controls on expenditures and decision making.

The Latin American research has been particularly enlightening on this subject, demonstrating that rational choice and opportunity are significant factors in explaining corruption in the sector (Di Tella & Savedoff, 2001, pp. 2–26). The following briefly summarizes findings on opportunity from these studies:

▶ A study in Peru identified a major problem with doctors working a second job in the private sector while rostered on at a public hospital (Alcazar & Andrade in Di Tella & Savedoff, 2001, pp. 123–161). Survey data from doctors found that, for tenured doctors in the public system, the rewards of absenteeism from their primary employment were considered to be high in light of both relatively low salaries and low risks of detection and dismissal.

▶ A survey of hospital staff in Bogota found that 'deficient supervisory and control mechanisms' were considered to be the main cause of the problem of doctor absenteeism by 46 per cent of respondents and the main cause of theft by 60 per cent (Giedon et al. in Di Tella & Savedoff, 2001, p. 187).

▶ In Venezuela, survey findings indicated that very low probabilities of detection and sanctioning strongly influenced the high rates of theft and absenteeism in public hospitals (Jaen & Paravisini in Di Tella & Savedoff, 2001, pp. 57–94).

The Latin American studies also found that, on the whole, low wages tended not to predict participation in corruption. This is not always the case in the corruption literature. The association between wages and corruption is variable in different studies, and there is evidence that higher wages can be associated with more corruption. For example, the finding in the Venezuelan study that well-paid health officials often engaged in corruption is confirmation of 'opinions expressed among key informants that corrupt officials bribe their way into jobs that provide opportunities for illicit gain. The high salary is simply another aspect of the corruption, which combines appointment, pay, and graft' (Di Tella & Savedoff, 2001, p. 23).

10.1057/9781137335098

Intervention impact studies

The above accounts of corruption-related issues in the health sector entail a number of obvious reforms that need to be enacted to minimize or entirely prevent corruption and improve public confidence. For example, there needs to be a complete ban on offering and accepting any type of gift or benefit from pharmaceutical companies or other companies seeking to do business with health services (Cohen in Transparency International, 2006, pp. 77–85). Regulators also have to be completely independent of regulated entities, entailing complete bans on gifts or financial support, while full disclosure of all conflicts of interest in medical research should be mandatory (Kassirer in Transparency International, 2006, pp. 85–91).

Furthermore, integrity-related reforms in health care need to occur within the legal and institutional frameworks set out in Chapters 4 and 5 of this book, including by bringing public health systems under the jurisdiction of anti-corruption commissions. The potential for large-scale procurement corruption in health also needs to be addressed through the specific measures set out in Chapter 7 – including through systematic responses to warning flags at all stages of the procurement process, and through the adoption of integrity pacts, corruption vulnerability assessments, and e-procurement where feasible.

Policy makers and managers in the health sector concerned with designing and testing tailor-made anti-corruption controls can also learn from implementation studies. Some promising results have been reported by Miller and Vian (2010) in regard to strategies designed to curb the 'corruption tax' on health services. In public hospitals in Albania and Kyrgyzstan, where co-payments were required, patient surveys indicated that informal payments were reduced by requirements that all transactions were receipted and signage be displayed listing prices. However, in the Kyrgyzstan case study there was some evidence of displacement to increased graft in the nominally free services. In Armenia, the government achieved some success in bypassing demands for informal payments by giving women vouchers for free maternal care and reimbursing hospitals by receipting the vouchers.

The Latin American studies also include a number of instructive intervention studies of varying depth. One example from Chile concerned innovation in the purchasing system for pharmaceuticals and medical supplies where alleged corruption and inefficiency in a centralized system contributed to marked asymmetries in prices and poor value for money. In the mid-1990s, the role of the government agency CENABAST was changed from being a monopoly purchaser of drugs to a 'mediator' agency for purchases by hospitals. The internet was used for the submission of tenders, and information about all tenders was posted on the web (see the section on e-procurement in Chapter 7 of this book). This introduced transparency into a previously opaque system and facilitated fair competition. In a partial impact assessment, Cohen and Montoya (2001) reported that by 1997 it was estimated that hospitals were achieving savings of up to 7 per cent on previous costs, amounting to approximately US$4 million.

Gray-Molina et al. (in Di Tella & Savedoff, 2001) provide a very brief account of a change in the management structure of hospitals in Bolivia, which allowed for new management committees to target procurement corruption. Reforms in the mid-1990s included the creation of local health directorates, which included community and local government representatives. Analysis across 30 hospitals of the prices of four common items revealed that prices were up to 40 per cent lower in hospitals with active local health directorates. This suggested that the partial devolution and democratization of hospital management contributed to reductions in suspected corruption in procurement through improvements in accountability and scrutiny of purchasing processes.

The application of price differentials to measuring suspected corruption and measuring the impact of reforms was also apparent in an initiative by the City Government of Buenos Aires, including the use of data in a time-series format. Concerned about corruption in procurement, the Health Secretariat undertook an experiment and started to record prices paid (Savedoff, 2007, p. 1).

The introduction of the system was announced in August 1996 and the first monthly data were collected in the same month. The price information was first reported back to hospital procurement managers in October. Researchers calculated average monthly prices, and also the monthly averages of the coefficient of variation (a measure of the dispersion of prices). Data were obtained for 17 months. Soon after the announcement of the scheme, average prices fell from an index figure of approximately 1.41 to approximately 1.24, and stayed around the lower level for five months (Schargrodsky et al. in Di Tella & Savedoff, 2001, pp. 95–122). At the time of the announcement of the scheme in August 1996 the coefficient was put at approximately 0.55. There was a dramatic fall over a two-month period to approximately 0.15. Following implementation of the scheme in October, the coefficient remained around the 0.2 mark for 10 months.

The researchers argued that the best interpretation of these data was that procurement officers involved in corruption responded immediately to the scheme's announcement by reducing some of the inflationary effects of bribes in advance of the scheme's implementation (see also Savedoff, 2007). The collection and circulation of price data then helped to keep prices – and variations in prices – at the lower rates.

Subsequently, however, the data evidenced regression. In February 1997, average prices rose and then stayed at a rate between the initial high point and the lowest point, trending down slightly. In August, the coefficient also rose somewhat and then began to trend down slowly. The researchers interpreted these developments as indicating that procurement officers discovered the new policy was not backed up with any enforcement. Consequently, they returned to their corrupt practices, albeit at a lower level than before. This outcome provides further evidence for the opportunity perspective on public health corruption outlined above:

> Procurement officers became accustomed to the process of reporting and noted the absence of consequences for 'poor performance.' In other words, revealing that a particular hospital was overpaying for certain supplies had led to no investigations, reprimands, or additional scrutiny. In the absence of such consequences, it is probable that corrupt individuals resumed their prior illicit activities. (Savedoff, 2007, p. 2)

Learning from the Buenos Aires case study

The Buenos Aires implementation study provides useful lessons consistent with the principles set out in previous sections of this book on measuring corruption and designing corruption prevention strategies and systems. Firstly, it is usually difficult to obtain objective pre-intervention baseline data for corruption. Nonetheless, this is not an insurmountable obstacle. As we have seen, useful indicators can be developed and obtained by consistent means over time. It is particularly beneficial if the indicators relate to very specific types or areas of corruption, such as purchase prices for medical goods in hospitals. This is consistent with the focus in situational crime prevention on discrete crimes and locations, and with analysis within the TASP framework. In the case of large differences in prices for medical supplies, there should be a safe assumption that initial prices are inflated if there are other indicators of corruption in the system, such as public or stakeholder opinion and media accounts. These data can then be used to track the likely impacts of anti-corruption interventions – other factors being held constant.

Ideally, pre-intervention data will go back far enough in time to show a clear trend. Unfortunately, for reasons not disclosed, this approach was not adopted in the Buenos Aires case study. However, there was a clear delineation of the point in time when full project implementation was complete. It appears that the scheme was fully implemented within one month. Knowing when an intervention is fully implemented – or when different phases are complete – allows for development of a more accurate interrupted time-series format.

It was also clear that the Buenos Aires anti-corruption project was very weak – in that enforcement was not just lacking but entirely absent. In the language of situational crime prevention, the process of collecting and circulating purchase prices was consistent with techniques of strengthening formal surveillance, alerting conscience and reducing anonymity. However, when it was clear that these were insufficient to sustain the crime prevention effect, there was no follow-through to tougher measures in areas such as increasing risks, reducing rewards and denying benefits. In the language of smart regulation, there was a failure to move up the enforcement pyramid from a form of assisted self-regulation towards proper investigations, issuing warnings and prosecuting suspects under administrative or criminal law. Furthermore, adoption of a full evaluative SCP or action research model would have meant that the relapses revealed by the data were addressed through follow-up diagnostics and implementation of additional measures.

Public health represents another area of considerable vulnerability to corruption and fraud, with potentially dire consequences for many vulnerable people. Findings on the extent of corruption in this area are highly variable, as is the norm with international estimates of corruption. But what is clear is that public health is a high-risk area for diverse types of illicit conduct. Variation is indicative that some systems are better than other in preventing corruption. Furthermore, the chapter's assessment of case studies of the implementation of anti-corruption measures is promising. Nonetheless, the assessment showed that processes for evaluating anti-corruption initiatives tend to be piecemeal and limited. To optimize

10.1057/9781137335098

reform, implementation of the full SCP model allows for modifications to anti-corruption strategies, including through increased enforcement, which should be tracked with the time-series data.

Overall it would seem that there is still some distance to go in building up a comprehensive body of evidence about effective corruption prevention in the health sector. While there are promising improvements in management and accountability in the sector, more effort needs to go into impact assessments.

10.1057/9781137335098

9
Designing out Corruption in Urban Planning

Abstract: *This final chapter focuses on an area of government decision making that is frequently associated with corruption. Corruption is often concentrated in local government in development application and approval processes. Using case studies, the chapter shows that the harmful effects of corruption in urban planning can be extremely serious, including in health and safety risks. Application of the TASP model demonstrates how procedural changes can be introduced into development approval processes that reduce corruption opportunities. Examples are provided from the recommendations of a major inquiry into corruption in one City Council.*

Graycar, Adam and Prenzler, Tim. *Understanding and Preventing Corruption.* Basingstoke: Palgrave Macmillan, 2013. DOI: 10.1057/9781137335098.

There is a significant body of literature devoted to designing out crime; its principles are described in Chapter 5 (Clarke, 1983, 2009; Clarke & Mayhew, 1980). The same principles can be applied to designing out corruption in urban planning.

Blocking criminal opportunities takes place by understanding place – its design and layout – and the different strategies that are appropriate for different parts of our built environment: houses, flats, shops, warehouses, factories, public transport, parks, pubs and so on. Public space contains risks, and the risks can be lessened by channelling movement patterns and dividing human activities into smaller and more manageable chunks.

'Place', however, is shaped and affected by planning decisions, and urban amenity requires good town planning. In addition to fostering unsafe communities, poor planning can result in limited transport options, and increased reliance on private cars over public transport or walking, insufficient health-related or educational opportunities, overcrowding, ugly or inappropriate buildings, environmentally inappropriate structures and damage to the environment.

Planning processes that mitigate these can be compromised by poor professionalism, political pressure and corruption. Corruption has played a role in many planning decisions. In New South Wales, Australia, the Independent Commission against Corruption receives about 3,000 complaints per year; of these 31 per cent are about local government, though not all are about urban planning (ICAC various Annual Reports). This is the largest volume of complaints by sector or function (three times the volume of those received about custodial services, which ranks second). Seven of the 30 public inquiries held between 2009 and 2012 have involved local councils, and some of these are discussed below.

In a study published in the USA over 30 years ago, and pertinently entitled *Decisions for Sale: Corruption and Reform in Land-use and Building Regulation*, Gardiner and Lyman (1978) documented their findings on local corruption. Based on eight compelling case studies, the book reported that in one city, corruption led to substantial but inadequately planned development in which the community could not provide schools, streets, water and recreational facilities. In another, corruption led to the construction of shoddy homes, many with high fire and safety risks.

In Chicago the authors revealed (ch. 6) that corruption in the rezoning process doubled the price paid for parkland, and that corruption in inspections led to approval of buildings with fire, health and safety hazards. In New York (ch. 8) corruption involving payoffs by architects, engineers, contractors and building owners added considerably to the price of apartments. In Cincinnati (ch. 9) corruption led to rigged bidding, shoddy construction and inflated costs which left homeowners with incomplete work, and taxpayers had to bail them out.

The nature of corrupt activities ranges from accepting a few dollars to looking the other way during a routine inspection, to getting approval for construction that does not meet standards, to buying information about future land zoning, to building developments where communities don't want them because there is insufficient infrastructure or potential for environmental damage.

The challenge is formidable. If we know corruption exists, but do not know how much or where, then how can preventive measures be put in place that do not tie up all concerned with massive amounts of red tape? The way forward is to examine and try to draw lessons from some recent cases. In order to illustrate, six short vignettes follow.

Wollongong: collapse of planning principles

In the 2000s the Independent Commission against Corruption in New South Wales investigated a systematically corrupt planning process in Wollongong, a coastal city south of Sydney (ICAC NSW, 2008). Beth Morgan was a senior town planner at Wollongong Council. Wishing to leave the council and establish a private consulting business, she pursued a series of sexual relationships with Wollongong developers, to integrate herself into their circle and establish them as clients of her potential firm. While doing so, she also wrote the Council's guidelines on ethical dealings with investors.

In the mid-2000s Morgan approved, without appropriate delegation, a $100-million-dollar development that did not meet the requirements of the Environmental or Town Plans established by the Council. She also reduced the fees payable to the Council by 10 per cent ($85,000). Her approvals breached height and floor space regulations, and she authorized the rezoning of prime land to benefit one of the developers. She had relationships with three developers who had applications with the Council and who all gave her gifts, many thousands of dollars in cash, and an offer to purchase, at below market value, a residence in one of the developments which she had approved.

10.1057/9781137335098

While Morgan escaped charges relating to the scandal after a two-year Department of Public Prosecutions inquiry found insufficient evidence, the three-volume ICAC investigation of the case alleged that Morgan failed to disclose the gifts, and outlined her many conflicts of interest. Not only was she and one of the developers found to have engaged in serious corrupt conduct, the whole Wollongong City Council was dismissed as a result of the ICAC findings, Part 3 of the ICAC report, made public on 8 October 2008, contained corrupt conduct findings in respect to the planner, two property developers, three of the planner's superiors at the Council, and four former Councillors.

The types of corruption exhibited here, as outlined in the TASP framework (Chapter 1), were abuse of discretion, conflict of interest, trading in influence, cronyism and bribery.

Aboriginal Land Council custodians

In February 2012 the ICAC conducted an investigation into corrupt land dealings involving the Wagonga Local Aboriginal Land Council (LALC). This Council is based in Narooma on the south coast of New South Wales. The estimated value of the land vested in the Wagonga LALC is between $3 million and $4 million (ICAC NSW, 2012b).

Between March 2005 and 2010, Ron Mason (the former chairperson of the Wagonga LALC), Vanessa Mason and Ken Foster (the former coordinator of the Wagonga LALC) received financial benefits from a developer in return for their facilitating negotiations in relation to a joint venture agreement between the LALC and Ron Medich Developments Pty Ltd. The essence was that very valuable land, much of it beachfront, would be developed for considerable profit.

Payments were made to the Council leaders: Ron Mason ($38,300), Ken Foster ($31,300) and Vanessa Mason ($127,746). The 99-year leases that were signed and facilitated by leaders contained extremely favourable benefits to the developers and were drawn up without the due process required by the rules of the Land Council. Developing the land in this way may not have been in the best interests of the community. The ICAC found that all the persons named here engaged in corrupt conduct and recommended prosecution for offences of misconduct in public office (Ron Mason, Vanessa Mason and Ken Foster) and offences of aiding and abetting the provision of corrupt benefits (Ron Medich).

10.1057/9781137335098

The types of corruption exhibited here were bribery, self-dealing, abuse of discretion and conflict of interest.

Money in an envelope

On 6 August 2008, the Pyo Family Trust lodged an application in relation to property owned by Strathfield Council (New South Wales). The Council subsequently decided to enter into negotiations with the Pyo Family Trust to conclude a licence agreement. Significant financial benefits would flow to the Pyo Family Trust in the event the negotiations settled on terms proposed by Mr Pyo (ICAC NSW, 2010b).

On 2 December 2009, Pyo gave an envelope to a Council officer to be given to the Council's General Manager. The envelope contained a Christmas card, a handwritten note and $2,000 in cash. In sending $2,000 to the General Manager Pyo intended, or expected, that he would keep the money for his personal use and in return, if necessary, use his position as to assist Pyo to achieve a favourable outcome to the licence agreement negotiations.

The General Manager immediately reported the offer of cash to ICAC, and ICAC conducted an investigation which resulted in the prosecution of Pyo. He pleaded not guilty to one count of corruptly offering an inducement and in the Local Court the charge was subsequently dismissed.

The corruption type alleged here was bribery.

Three vignettes from New Jersey

Turning from Australia to the USA, recent examples of corruption in planning issues can be identified in three New Jersey cities within an hour's drive of each other.

Tony Mack, Mayor of Trenton, the capital city of New Jersey, was arrested on 10 September 2012 for offering to sell city land for construction of a car park. A television news clip showed how patently unsuitable the land would have been for this purpose. There was no suggestion of any planning process. The land was valued at $271,000. And it was alleged that Mack would sell it to the developer for $200,000, and reported that it fetched only $100,000. He and his two associates were to split the profits

(CBS News, 2012; Huffington Post, 2012). At the time of writing there had been no trial, and thus these are only accusations, as yet untested in court.

Interestingly this followed a case just three years earlier. In July 2009 Hoboken Mayor Peter Cammarano, who had been in office for just 23 days, was arrested for taking bribes. During that brief period he was filmed three times taking payments totalling $25,000 to push through building plans for a high-rise development in Hoboken. Details of the indictment can be read at http://blog.nj.com/ledgerupdates_impact/2009/07/Mayor-Cammarano-Schaffer.pdf. Cammarano was sentenced in August 2010 to two years in federal prison (*New York Times*, 6 August 2010).

This followed the conviction and sentencing, less than a year before, of Sharpe James to 27 months in prison. James had been mayor of New Jersey's largest city, Newark, for 21 years and was alleged to have engaged in many corrupt practices (Tuttle, 2009). His trial and conviction, according to the *New York Times*, 'covered a host of urban touchstones, from sex to mayoral power to developable real estate' (17 April 2008). He was accused and convicted of helping his girlfriend (Tamika Riley) gain access to a city-sponsored programme meant to redevelop Newark's struggling neighbourhoods. At issue were nine city-owned properties Riley bought through the programme, for which she paid a total of $46,000 and resold quickly for a profit of more than $600,000. Prosecutors argued that James used his influence as mayor to help her consummate the deals. Riley, who was convicted of tax evasion and lying about her income to collect housing subsidies, was sentenced to 15 months in prison.

In these New Jersey examples the types of corrupt behaviour included bribery, misappropriation, conflict of interest, abuse of discretion, cronyism, trading in influence and pay to play.

All six cases show that opportunity for corrupt behaviour is often present, and that process can be disregarded for greed. As outlined in Chapter 2, corruption takes on varying dynamics. There are bribes and benefits that are *extorted* from people so that they might receive a benefit or a service to which they are entitled, but are being denied. On the other hand, principals and agents *collude* with one another in order to evade rules, regulations and processes to the advantage of the principal, with the agent willingly accepting the payment. In all our cases above there has been collusion rather than extortion. When there is collusion it is in the interest of all parties to keep the matter secret, since they see it as a win–win situation. This makes detection and prevention harder than it is for many (regular) crimes.

10.1057/9781137335098

Prevention and design

The second analytical framework comes from crime prevention theory (Chapter 5), which can provide guidance in designing out corruption in local government. Every corruption opportunity, like every crime, requires three ingredients: a motivated offender, a suitable target and the absence of a capable guardian (Felson, 2002). So, to design out corruption the first step is to identify the potential offenders, targets and guardians.

The potential *offenders* in these cases are the shady developers, the professionals who do not act professionally, and elected officials who put their own interests ahead of those of the community that they are meant to serve, as well as custodians of traditional land who are prepared to compromise its use.

For developers the risk factors in their activities are the desire to use scarce land for maximum profit, the wish to speed up an application and get something approved that is of questionable value to the community. Their opportunities lie in developing relationships with elected officials, town planning staff and corruptible officials, and exploiting processes that are vulnerable to manipulation.

The professionals exhibit risk factors when they show lack of professionalism and expose themselves to regulatory capture. They are motivated sometimes by friendship or love, but most often by greed. In essence their emotion or greed overrides their professionalism. Their opportunities lie in lack of supervision, extensive discretion, no performance standards or standards that are not adhered to.

The elected officials are at risk when greed or political ambition drive their decision making, and their opportunities lie in working closely with officials engaged in day-to-day planning work.

The *targets* are the planning authorities who make decisions about urban amenities and of course the residents who enjoy those amenities. The targets normally expect that decisions made about land use will ensure a safe and habitable urban environment, though there are many debates about zoning, not just in local government but in controversial fields such as the zoning of farming land for oil, coal or gas exploration, or permitting logging in old-growth forest.

A *guardian* keeps an eye on the potential target of a crime. It entails the presence of a human element to look out and deter (Hollis et al., 2013). The capable guardian in these situations are the colleagues and those whose work embeds the process and the culture. In most of the cases sketched out above, there was a failure to see the corruption. In Wollongong the conflict of interest was rampant; in New Jersey it was plain criminal. In the Aboriginal Land Council case there was the abuse of trust and discretion, and an inability to hold custodians to account.

Applying the framework to Wollongong

Here we shall take Wollongong (ICAC NSW, 2008, pp. 120–139) as an exemplary case. The targets, as indicated above, are the City Council and, ultimately, the residents of Wollongong. The opportunities for the offenders are shaped by:

- valuable land close to the central business district of a large coastal regional city;
- inappropriate and unlawful reliance on SEPP 1 (a mechanism in NSW enabling variance in development standards contained within environmental planning instruments) to authorize significant departures from development standards in relation to height and floor space ratios;
- a number of relatively frequent major development applicants with recurring contact with town planning staff, the General Manager and Councillors.

The absence of capable guardians can be summarized as follows:

- a relative shortage of town planning staff and managers able to determine a large volume of development applications, some of which were complex;
- a Local Environmental Plan, to which colleagues could refer, that was out of date;
- a General Manager with a strong pro-development philosophy which he allowed to prevail over his duty to ensure that development applications were being assessed and processed according to law;
- a Council that could not or would not require the General Manager to account for decisions taken with respect to major development applications.

10.1057/9781137335098

A categorization of *opportunities* has been developed in the literature (Graycar & Sidebottom, 2012). It identifies both systemic opportunities and localized opportunities for corruption. It can be applied here.

In the Wollongong case the following systemic opportunities were observed:

- ▶ lack of culture of integrity within the whole organization and its stakeholders/clients (developers);
- ▶ lack of integrity among leaders;
- ▶ patronage and cronyism accepted;
- ▶ complexity of regulations and of systems;
- ▶ weak institutions of governance;
- ▶ ethical codes do not exist, or are not enforced.

The following localized opportunities were also observed:

- ▶ strong demand for waterfront property where demand exceeds supply;
- ▶ planners had specialized knowledge and extensive discretion;
- ▶ their decisions affected the costs and benefits of activities;
- ▶ the activity of planners was remote from supervision;
- ▶ supervision and oversight were not taken seriously;
- ▶ conflict of interest was disregarded;
- ▶ insufficient protections – absence of capable guardian;
- ▶ low decision monitoring;
- ▶ low risk of being caught.

Once opportunities are identified, and corruption activities classified (as per TASP, above), a set of controls can be implemented.

In situational crime prevention, there are four basic types of approaches promulgated by Clarke (1995, 2009) which are applicable here:

- ▶ Increase the effort required to behave corruptly
- ▶ Increase the risks of corrupt behaviour
- ▶ Reduce the rewards of corrupt behaviour
- ▶ Remove excuses for corrupt behaviour

Under each of these headings we can identify general interventions for corruption reduction. We also give for each of them a couple of specific examples taken from the context of corruption in Wollongong. The Wollongong applications below are derived from the ICAC NSW report (2008).

10.1057/9781137335098

Increase the effort required to behave corruptly

In general:

- ▶ Establish effective internal and external reporting procedures
- ▶ Ensure that the decision-making process is transparent and subject to regular and random audits
- ▶ Rotate agents
- ▶ Create a code of ethics
- ▶ Modify guidelines for conflicts of interest
- ▶ Rotate staff in and out of decision-making roles
- ▶ For larger applications, always have two officers working on the processing of the application, and make agreement of both a condition of approval
- ▶ Reduce the decision maker's discretion, which limits the 'space' in which to act corruptly
- ▶ Publish expected timelines for processing, and set performance indicators that staff need to meet in that respect
- ▶ External auditing for party finances and campaigns

ICAC NSW also made recommendations specific to Wollongong, as follows. For a two-year period the Council should not be able to depart from development standards by more than 10 per cent. The New South Wales Minister for Planning should consider ways in which Joint Regional Planning Panels can be made resistant to improper influence, such as: regularly rotating panel members across different panels, limiting the tenure of panel members, and drawing panel members on a random basis or at least in a manner which makes their appointment difficult to predict. The Wollongong City Council should allocate incoming development applications to town planners with no regard to the wishes of applicants.

Increase the risks of corrupt behaviour

In general:

- ▶ Set and enforce guidelines for approvals, and require a transparent process for deviation from guidelines
- ▶ Develop appropriate oversight mechanisms for discretionary decision making

10.1057/9781137335098

▸ Introduce random third-party reviews of applications for decision-making integrity and consistency

▸ Implement an appeals mechanism which makes it more likely that corrupt behaviour will be discovered

▸ Establish workplace performance indicators

▸ Introduce random integrity testing

▸ Make known that criminal penalties may apply

▸ Ensure mechanisms for the protection of whistleblowers, and let it be known (culturally) that whistleblowing is OK

▸ Develop a set of transparency practices, and welcome vigilant media and civil society oversight

ICAC's recommendations specific to Wollongong were as follows. The Wollongong City Council should publish, on its website, a register of development application determinations (including approvals and refusals) that rely on SEPP 1 (or its equivalent). The New South Wales Department of Planning should monitor and enforce the requirements for all consent authorities to keep records of their assessment of all development applications which seek a variation to development standards. The Wollongong City Council should examine officers' access to and use of files as part of its regular internal audit programme. The Wollongong City Council's Audit and Governance Committee should be reconstituted to include additional external membership and an independent chairperson. The Council's Internal Ombudsman should have direct access to the Committee and the independent chairperson.

Reduce the rewards of corrupt behaviour

In general:

▸ Immediately dismiss any application that was the object of corrupt acts or attempted corrupt acts – dismiss or put on hold first, explore later

▸ Revoke planning permission for developments arising from corrupt decisions

▸ In extreme cases, seek orders for demolition or seek to impose prohibitive taxes

▸ Develop and enforce penalties for breaches

10.1057/9781137335098

These were ICAC's recommendations specific to Wollongong. The Director General of the Department of Planning should actively use the power to revoke or modify his or her assumed concurrence to prevent abuse of SEPP 1 (or its equivalent) by all consent authorities. Internal Wollongong City Council information relating to the possible rezoning of land should be released publicly as soon as possible but in accordance with section 66(3) of the Environmental Planning and Assessment Act.

Remove excuses for corrupt behaviour

In general:

▸ Do not allow precedents so that previous poor behaviour which may have been tolerated is used as an excuse for new bad behaviour
▸ 'Name and shame' all persons found to be engaged in behaviour which breaches specified codes of conduct
▸ Establish and enforce codes of conducts that apply to persons submitting applications to Council
▸ Increase the moral cost of corruption
▸ Create a culture of integrity

ICAC's recommendations specific to Wollongong were as follows. The Wollongong City Council should rewrite the position descriptions, contracts and performance agreements of the General Manager and relevant senior managers so that the desired anti-corruption behaviour is defined, recognized and rewarded. It should re-establish the position of Internal Ombudsman. It should amend its Code of Conduct to include a prohibition on binding caucus votes in relation to development applications. The NSW Minister for Planning should consider expanding the classes of development for which Joint Regional Planning Panels will be the consent authority to include certain categories of development relying on SEPP 1 objections. The Wollongong City Council should determine clear, objective and auditable criteria for deciding which development applications are referred to the Independent Hearing and Assessment Panel.

In conclusion, corrupt behaviour has been a feature of urban development for a long time, and in many settings and places. Pessimists say it is too deeply entrenched for things to change. Yet change can indeed come about if some of the suggestions above are put to an empirical test.

10.1057/9781137335098

First, clearly identify and categorize the corrupt behaviour using the TASP model. Then a mixture of ethical development, integrity building, criminalization and penalties, and situational prevention can make inroads into the assumption that the high and powerful can corruptly manipulate the urban environment and damage urban amenity. One approach, rooted in situational crime prevention, can provide tools which might limit corrupt behaviour in urban planning.

10.1057/9781137335098

Postscript

The past few decades have seen major innovations and improvements in public sector integrity management strategies around the world. At the same time, corruption constitutes a significant ongoing and damaging phenomenon in many places. There is a great deal of work still to be done in addressing the problem, and this book supports this mission by helping to clarify the nature and causes of corruption and focus attention on 'what works' in stopping the onset and continuation of corruption.

▶ In writing this book, we have sought to challenge fatalistic notions that corruption is endemic and therefore inevitable in human society. Despite the apparent pervasiveness of corruption, there is also significant variation, and this is a major source of evidence against a fatalistic attitude. Country variations include many extremes. As shown in the book, there are countries that suffer from chronic corruption and the problem often seems to be intractable. However, there are other countries with extremely low levels of corruption indicators. In some cases, most notably the Scandinavian countries, it appears that cultural factors play a critical part in this, and that a culture of public integrity means a relatively simple anti-corruption infrastructure is sufficient to maintain standards. In other cases, more sophisticated systems had to be introduced to reduce corruption and then keep it at low levels. Initial change has often been driven by scandal and adverse publicity, including high profile cases of major corruption. Hong Kong and Australia are examples of this experience. In these cases, anti-corruption commissions have played

10.1057/9781137335098

a central role in reform through investigations and prosecutions, covert methods, integrity audits, and education and training programs.

The authors' home country of Australia provides something of a social laboratory and has seen positive changes in anti-corruption systems in the past quarter century. The establishment of the New South Wales Independent Commission Against Corruption in 1989 represents a dividing line between an overly simplistic and naïve approach to corruption and an increasingly complex pre-emptive approach, with many instructive experiences along the way. These developments have contributed to Australia's high rating on international corruption indices. However, corruption opportunities still remain, including in New South Wales, where recent scandals continue to sully the reputations of politicians, public servants and business people – as illustrated in a number of case studies in the book.

The Australian example shows that wealthy established democracies are by no means immune from corruption. Free and fair elections, an independent judiciary, a free press, and independent institutions like ombudsmen and auditors-general, are not sufficient on their own to deliver levels of probity that the public rightly expect. In many countries, this basic infrastructure requires refinement and modifications to enhance democracy and facilitate corruption prevention. Examples include rules around disclosures of political donations, and prohibitions on politicians and public servants receiving gifts. At the same time, many jurisdictions require additional protections. A specialist anti-corruption agency is the exemplar add-on institution that can contribute significantly to combating corruption given the right powers, resources and political support.

The academic literature concerned with understanding and preventing corruption has made a valuable contribution to informed practice, and to education and training in public sector integrity management. At the same time, academic publications can often be theoretically and statistically complex and, consequently, difficult to digest for many readers. There is also a large practitioner-oriented literature, focused on promoting summary guidelines, mainly produced by anti-corruption agencies and NGOs. More theory and more empirical research would make this literature more comprehensive. In this book we have sought to navigate a middle course between theory and practice. Theoretical perspectives on the causes and prevention of corruption have been introduced where they help in understanding the problem and in designing systems and strategies that are most likely to be effective. We have also developed clear sets

10.1057/9781137335098

of guidelines for preventing corruption based on case study diagnostics and the findings of intervention studies.

Perhaps the most important lesson from this book is that effective corruption prevention relies on a process that matches interventions to risks. In other words, anti-corruption strategies should be fit-for-purpose and match the particular problems and conditions that apply in different settings. This is one of the key lessons of situational crime prevention that is directly applicable to corruption prevention. Situational prevention emphasizes the importance of understanding opportunity factors and shutting down opportunities, as far as possible. This can be achieved by deploying a range of techniques that increase the effort and risk, and reduce the rewards, for would-be participants in a corrupt transaction. Available techniques include setting and communicating rules, increasing surveillance and guardianship, denying benefits and facilitating compliance. But situational crime prevention does not advocate an off-the-shelf application of all possible techniques. Instead, it emphasizes the importance of site-specific diagnostic research, and an experimental or quasi-experimental approach to implementing strategies, monitoring effects and making adjustments. The book also introduced the TASP model of analysis to show how the categories of 'Types, Activities, Sectors and Places' can be used to analyse corruption and develop workable prevention strategies.

Finding the most appropriate and effective mix of strategies is also a key lesson from the literature on regulatory theory. In particular, the concept of smart regulation emphasizes how a data-rich approach is most likely to be effective, especially in demonstrating the impacts of different strategies, and demonstrating effectiveness within a context of democratic accountability. Obtaining stakeholder advice and feedback is part of this approach in engaging regulated bodies in a responsive regulatory process. Theory in this area also helps focus attention on the need to ensure anti-corruption strategies do not impede basic service provision or create inefficiencies into government processes. An optimal integrity system should in fact facilitate productivity and support prosperity by eliminating the unproductive diversion of taxpayer funds into private hands.

Obtaining measures of the nature and extent of corruption is therefore an essential element of corruption prevention. Chapter 3 argued that the best way to mitigate the problem of indeterminacy in measurement is by triangulating as many indicators as possible. Public and insider perception and experience surveys have been particularly important sources of information, providing valuable benchmarks with which to assess regulatory impacts by tracking changes over time. International surveys have also provided an indispensable benchmarking framework and help focus attention on underperforming jurisdictions.

An international approach to corruption should not, however, be overly stigmatizing. Sharing experiences and challenges can be productive to all parties with different types of corruption issues. International inspections and delegations across the spectrum of rich and poor countries can add to the objectivity and quality of integrity assessments and advice. International treaties also provide basic standards and guidelines, and provide a key reference point for keeping pressure on governments to address corruption problems.

We have sought to develop these themes in the final four chapters by showing how they apply to different types of corruption in different settings. Criminal justice was chosen because it is an area where corruption might be considered anathema to practitioners, yet it has seen chronic corruption even in the most advanced democratic nations. Judicial corruption is particularly shocking, yet one of the lessons from experience in this area is that judges and magistrates should be subject to anti-corruption procedures as much as any occupation. Processes of scandal and reform across the police, judiciary and corrections illustrate that significant improvements can be made from a very low base. The application of video-recording is one example of a common and fairly simple technology being used to reduce opportunities in areas highly vulnerable to misconduct.

The chapter on corruption prevention in procurement highlighted methods used by unscrupulous suppliers and public servants to exploit system vulnerabilities. However, the analysis showed that these opportunities are susceptible to closure. Rule setting and surveillance are particularly important for creating a level playing field and ensuring the public benefits from the right quality and lowest cost supply of goods and services to government.

The chapter on public health services reported on a number of exemplar natural experiments in corruption prevention. The results were mixed, but there are sufficient positive results on the record, especially from a series of studies carried out in Latin America, to show that a variety of quite simple opportunity reducing measures can be introduced into health systems, particularly in the area of procurement of medical supplies by hospitals.

The final chapter was concerned with an area of government action that is often closest in its effects to ordinary people and one which has

10.1057/9781137335098

also been commonly associated with corruption. Local government may have a bad history of malfeasance but, again, misconduct is not universal in the sector. The case studies in corrupt urban planning decision-making showed there are counter-measures which can be applied to close off corruption opportunities and clean up local government.

As noted, in planning and writing this book we deliberately wrote for a non-specialist audience and sought to address a gap that we saw in the literature. We are hopeful the book will be read by academic colleagues and students in educational institutions. But we are most keen for the book to serve as a handy reference source and guide to action for politicians, political party officials, research and policy officers, and for other people working in applied settings: corporate and union leaders, investigators and prosecutors, legal advisors, complaints officers, and corruption prevention and education officers. We are keen to hear from practitioners about the relevance of the book and readers' experiences in the global fight against corruption.

10.1057/9781137335098

References

Abramoff, J. (2012). I know the Congressional culture of corruption. *The Atlantic*, July/August 2012. http://www.theatlantic.com/politics/archive/2012/07/i-know-the-congressional-culture-of-corruption/260081/

Andersson, S. & Heywood, P. M. (2009). The politics of perception: use and abuse of Transparency International's approach to measuring corruption. *Political Studies*, 57(4), 746–767.

Anechiarico, F., & Jacobs, J. B. (1996). *The pursuit of absolute integrity: how corruption control makes government ineffective*. Chicago: University of Chicago Press.

Ayres, I., & Braithwaite, J. (1992). *Responsive regulation: transcending the deregulation debate*. New York: Oxford University Press.

Birch, S. (2012). *Electoral malpractice*. Oxford: Oxford University Press.

Branstetter, J. (2005). *The Darleen Druyan debacle: procurement, power and corruption*. George Washington University School of Law. Retrieved from http://www.dtic.mil/cgi-bin/GetTRDoc?AD=ADA437374

Brooks, G., Button, M. & Gee, J. (2012). The scale of health-care fraud: a global evaluation. *Security Journal*, 25(1), 76–87.

Brown, A., & Head, B. (2005). Assessing integrity systems. *Australian Journal of Public Administration*, 64(2), 42–47.

CBS News (2012). Mayor Tony Mack arrested 10 Sept. From http://www.cbsnews.com/8301-201_162-57509321/n.j-mayor-tony-mack-arrested-in-corruption-probe/

CCC WA (2008a). *Misconduct resistance: an integrated governance approach to protecting agency integrity.* Perth, http://www.ccc.wa.gov.au/SiteCollectionDocuments/CCC-MR-complete.pdf

CCC WA (2008b). *Public perceptions survey.* Perth, Corruption and Crime Commission, http://www.ccc.wa.gov.au/Publications/Reports/Documents/Published%20Reports/2008/public-perceptions-survey-2008-02-27.pdf

CCC WA (2011). *Report on the investigation of alleged public sector misconduct in relation to the purchase of toner cartridges in exchange for gifts outside government procurement policies and arrangements.* Perth: Corruption and Crime Commission.

Clarke, R. V., & Mayhew, P. (1980). *Designing out crime.* London: HM Stationery Office.

Clarke, R. V. (1983). Situational crime prevention: its theoretical basis and practical scope. *Crime and Justice, 4*, 225–256.

Clarke, R. V. (1995). Situational crime prevention. *Crime & Justice, 19*, 91.

Clarke, R. V. (1997). *Situational crime prevention: successful case studies* Guilderland, NY: Harrow and Heston.

Clarke, R. V. (2008). Situational crime prevention. In R Wortley & L Mazerolle (Eds.), *Environmental criminology and crime analysis.* Cullompton: Willan.

Clarke, R. V. (2009). Situational crime prevention: theoretical background and current practice. In M. D. Krohn, A. J. Lizotte & G. P. Hall (Eds.), *Handbook on crime and deviance* (pp. 259–276). London: Springer Science + Business Media.

CLEDS VIC (2007). *Standards for Victoria Police law enforcement data security* Melbourne, Commissioner for Law Enforcement Security, http://www.cleds.vic.gov.au/retrievemedia.asp?Media_ID=20338

CMC QLD (2011). *Public perceptions of the public service.* Brisbane, Crime and Misconduct Commission, http://www.cmc.qld.gov.au/research-and-publications/publications/research/public-perceptions/public-perceptions-of-the-public-service-findings-from-the-2010-public-attitudes-survey.pdf/view

Cohen, J. C., & Montoya, J. C. (2001). *Using technology to fight corruption in pharmaceutical purchasing: lessons learned from the Chilean experience.* Washington, World Bank, http://citeseerx.ist.psu.edu/viewdoc/summary?doi=10.1.1.196.2132

Cornish, D., & Clarke, C. (2003). Opportunities, precipitators and criminal decisions. In M. Smith & D. B. Cornish (Eds.), *Theory for situational crime prevention* (pp. 41–96). Monsey, NY: Criminal Justice Press.

Critchley, T. (2007). *A history of police in England and Wales (900–1966)*. London: Constable & Company.

de Graaf, G., & Huberts, L. (2008). Portraying the nature of corruption using an explorative case study design. *Public Administration Review*, July/August, 640–653.

de Sousa, L. (2010). Anti-corruption agencies: between empowerment and irrelevance. *Crime Law and Social Change, 53*(1), 5–22.

Della Porta, D., & Vannucci, A. (1999). *Corrupt exchanges: actors, resources, and mechanisms of political corruption*. New Brunswick: Transaction Publishers.

Di Tella, R., & Savedoff, W. D. (2001). *Diagnosis corruption: fraud in Latin America's public hospitals*. Washington: Inter-American Development Bank.

Dixon, D. (2006). "A Window into the Interviewing Process?" The audio-visual recording of police interrogation in New South Wales, Australia. *Policing and Society, 16*(4), 323–348.

DPIC (2013). *Innocence and the death penalty*. Washington, Death Penalty Information Center, http://deathpenaltyinfo.org/innocence-and-death-penalty

Ecenbarger, W. (2012). *Kids for cash: two judges, thousands of children and a $2.6 million kickback scheme*. New York: The New Press.

Ede, A., Homel, R., & Prenzler, T. (2002). Situational corruption prevention. In T. Prenzler & J. Ransley (Eds.), *Police reform: building integrity* (pp. 210–225). Sydney: Hawkins Press.

Ekblom, P. (1999). Can we make crime prevention adaptive by learning from other evolutionary struggles? *Studies on crime and crime prevention, 8*, 27–51.

Elliott, C. (2010). *White coast, black hat*. Boston: Beacon Press.

Etzioni, A. (1977). Human beings are not very easy to change after all. In J. D. Douglas & J. M. Johnson (Eds.), *Official deviance: readings in malfeasance, misfeasance, and other forms of corruption* (pp. 411–416). Philadelphia: Lippincott.

Felson, M. (2002). *Crime and everyday life*. Thousand Oaks, California: Sage Publications.

Felson, M. (2011). Corruption in the broad sweep of history. In A Graycar & R. G. Smith (Eds.), *Handbook of global research and practice in corruption* (pp. 12–17). Cheltenham, UK: Edward Elgar.

10.1057/9781137335098

Gardiner, J. A., & Lyman, T. R. (1978). *Decisions for sale: corruption and reform in land-use and building.* New York: Praeger.

Garrett, B. L. (2011). *Convicting the innocent: where criminal prosecutions go wrong.* Cambridge , M: Harvard University Press.

Gill Hearn, R. (2009, December 31). *DOI arrests 877 in 2009, continuing the agency's record-high trend of arrests.* Retrieved 22 July 2013, from http://www.nyc.gov/html/doi/downloads/pdf/133yearend12-31-2009.pdf.

Goldacre, B. (2012). *Bad pharma: how drug companies mislead doctors and harm patients.* Hammersmith: 4th Estate.

Gorta, A. (1998). Minimizing corruption: applying lessons from the crime prevention literature. *Crime, Law & Social Change, 30,* 67–87.

Gorta, A. (2006). Corruption risk areas and corruption resistance. In C. Sampford, A. Shacklock, C. Connors & F. Galtung (Eds.), *Measuring corruption* (pp. 203–219). Burlington VT: Ashgate.

Grabosky, P., & Braithwaite, J. (1986). *Of manners gentle: the enforcement strategies of Australian business regulatory agencies.* Melbourne: Oxford University Press.

Graycar, A., & Sidebottom, A. (2012). Corruption and control: a corruption reduction approach. *Journal of Financial Crime, 19*(4), 384–399.

Graycar, A., & Villa, D. (2011). The loss of governance capacity through corruption. *Governance: An International Journal of Policy, Administration, and Institutions, 24* (3), 419–438.

Gunningham, N., & Grabosky, P. (1998). *Smart regulation: designing environmental policy.* Oxford: Oxford University Press.

Gunson, P. (2006, August 17). Obituary: General Alfredo Stroessner: dictator who mastered the fixing of elections and made Paraguay a smugglers' paradise. *The Guardian,* p. 37.

Hansen, H. K. (2012). The power of performance indices in the global politics of anti-corruption. *Journal of International Relations and Development, 15*(4), 506–531.

Heilbrunn, J. R. (2004). *Anti-corruption commissions: panacea or real medicine to fight corruption?* Washington, World Bank Institute, siteresources.worldbank.org/WBI/Resources/wbi37234Heilbrunn.pdf

Heinrich, F., & Hodess, R. (2011). Measuring corruption. In Adam Graycar & Russell G. Smith (Eds.), *Handbook of global research and practice in corruption* (pp. 18–33). Cheltenham, UK: Edward Elgar.

HMSO UK (1993). *The Royal Commission on Criminal Justice: report.* London, http://www.official-documents.gov.uk/document/cm22/2263/2263.pdf

10.1057/9781137335098

Hollis, M. E., Felson, M., & Welch, B. (2013). The capable guardian in routine activities theory. *Crime prevention and community safety, 15*(1), 65–79.

Huberts, L., Lasthuizen, K., & Peeters, C. (2006). Measuring corruption: exploring the iceberg. In C. Sampford, A. Shacklock, C. Connors & F. Galtung (Eds.), *Measuring corruption* (pp. 266–293). Burlington VT: Ashgate.

Huffington Post (2012). Tony Mack arrested, from http://www. huffingtonpost.com/2012/09/10/tony-mack-arrested-trenton-mayor_n_1870266.html

ICAC Hong Kong (2011). *ICAC annual survey 2011: executive summary.* Hong Kong, Independent Commission Against Corruption, http:// www.icac.org.hk/filemanager/en/Content_1283/2011surveysummary. pdf

ICAC Hong Kong (2012). *2011 annual report.* Hong Kong, Independent Commission Against Corruption, http://www.icac.org.hk/ filemanager/gb/Content_1238/2011.pdf

ICAC Hong Kong (2013). *Best practice checklist: procurement.* Hong Kong: Corruption Prevention Department, Independent Commission Against Corruption, http://www.icac.org.hk/filemanager/en/ Content_1031/procurepractices.pdf

ICAC NSW (2006). *Community attitudes to corruption and the ICAC.* Sydney, Independent Commission Against Corruption, http:// www.icac.nsw.gov.au/documents/doc_download/1662-community-attitudes-to-corruption-and-the-icac-report-on-the-2006-survey

ICAC NSW (2008). *Report on an investigation into corruption allegations affecting Wollongong City Council* Sydney, ICAC, http://www.icac.nsw. gov.au/investigations/past-investigations/investigationdetail/65

ICAC NSW (2010a). *Community attitudes to corruption and the ICAC.* Sydney, Independent Commission Against Corruption,

ICAC NSW (2010b). *Investigation into the offer of a corrupt payment to an officer of Strathfield Municipal Council.* Sydney, ICAC, http://www.icac. nsw.gov.au/investigations/past-investigations/investigationdetail/162

ICAC NSW (2012a) *Annual report, 2011–12.* Sydney: Independent Commission Against Corruption.

ICAC NSW (2012b). *Investigation into the conduct of officers of the Wagonga Local Aboriginal Land Council and others* Sydney, ICAC, http://www.icac.nsw.gov.au/investigations/past-investigations/ investigationdetail/188

10.1057/9781137335098

ICAC NSW (2013). *Preventing corruption/knowing your risks/procurement.* Sydney, Independent Commission Against Corruption, http://www.icac.nsw.gov.au/preventing-corruption/knowing-your-risks/procurement/4305

Jauregui, B. (2007). Policing in northern India as a different kind of political science: ethnographic rethinking of normative 'political interference' in investigations and order maintenance. *Asian Policing,* 5(1), 15–48.

Johnston, M. (2005). *Syndromes of corruption: wealth, power, and democracy.* New York: Cambridge University Press.

Joutsen, M., & Graycar, A. (2012). When experts and diplomats agree: negotiating peer review of the UN Convention Against Corruption. *Global Governance, 18*(4), 425–439.

Joutsen, M., & Keranen, J. (2009). *Corruption and the prevention of corruption in Finland.* Helsinki: Ministry of Justice, Finland.

Kassin, S. M., Leo, R. A., Meissner, C. A., Richman, K D., Colwell, L. H., Leach, A. & La Fon, D. (2007). Police interviewing and interrogation: a self-report survey of police practices and beliefs. *Law and Human Behavior, 31*(4), 381–400.

Kernaghan, K., & Langford, J. W. (1990). *The responsible public servant.* Halifax NS: Institute for Research on Public Policy, Institute of Public Administration of Canada.

Khan, M., & Kaufmann, D. (2009). Does poverty cause corruption? Retrieved 17 January 2013, from http://developmentdrums.org/wp-content/uploads/DD20Transcript1.pdf

Kiley, S. (1997, September 9). Dictator with a taste for chaos and witchcraft. *The Times,* p. 13.

Klitgaard, R. E. (1988). *Controlling corruption.* Ewing: University of California Press.

Knutsson, J., & Kuhlhorn, E. (1997). Macro-measures against crime: the example of check forgeries. In E. Clarke (Ed.), *Situational crime prevention: successful case studies* (pp. 113–121). Guilderland, NY: Harrow and Heston.

Kuhlhorn, E. (1997). Housing allowances in a welfare society: reducing the temptation to cheat. In E. Clarke (Ed.), *Situational crime prevention: successful case studies* (pp. 235–241). Guilderland, NY: Harrow and Heston.

Lehoucq, F. (2003). Electoral fraud: causes, types, and consequences. *Annual Review of Political Science, 6,* 233–256.

10.1057/9781137335098

Lessig, L. (2011). *Republic, lost: how money corrupts Congress and a plan to stop it.* New York: Hachette.

Mauss, M. (1950). *The gift: the form and reason for exchange in archaic societies.* New York: W. W. Norton.

McAllister, I., & White, S. (2011). Public perceptions of electoral fairness in Russia. *Europe-Asia Studies, 63,* 663–683.

McAllister, I., Pietsch, J., & Graycar, A. (2012). ANU poll: perceptions of corruption and ethical conduct. Retrieved from http://politicsir.cass.anu.edu.au/polls-and-surveys/anupoll

McLean, B., & Elkind, P. (2004). *The smartest guys in the room: the amazing rise and scandalous fall of Enron.* London: Penguin.

Miller, K., & Vian, T. (2010). Strategies for reducing informal payments. In T. Vian, W. D. Savedoff & M. Mathisen (Eds.), *Anti-corruption in the health sector: strategies for transparency and accountability.* Sterling, VA: Stylus Publishing.

Mungiu-Pippidi, A. (2011). *Contextual choices in fighting corruption: lessons learned.* Norwegian Agency for Development Cooperation, http://www.norad.no/en/tools-andpublications/publications/evaluations/publication/_attachment/383807?_download=true&_ts=132ba328b0e

Naughton, M. (2012). The Criminal Cases Review Commission: innocence versus safety and the integrity of the criminal justice system. *Criminal Law Quarterly 58*(2), 207–244.

Nye, J. S. (1967). Corruption and political development: a cost-benefit analysis. *The American Political Science Review, 61*(2), 417–427.

OECD (2000). *Trust In government: ethics measures In OECD countries.* Paris, http://www.oecd.org/corruption/ethics/48994450.pdf

OECD (2009). *Towards a sound integrity framework: instruments, processes, structures and conditions for implementation.* Paris, http://search.oecd.org/officialdocuments/displaydocumentpdf/?doclanguage=en&cote=GOV/PGC/GF(2009)1

OECD (2013). *Specialised anti-corription institutions – review of models.* http://www.oecd.org/corruption/acn/specialisedanti-corruptioninstitutions-reviewofmodels.htm

Olken, B. A. (2007). Monitoring corruption: evidence from a field experiment in Indonesia. *Journal of Political Economy, 115*(2), 200–249.

Oxford Policy Management (2007). *Measuring corruption.* 2007-1, http://www.opml.co.uk/sites/opml/files/bn2007-01_0.pdf

Prenzler, T., & Faulkner, N. (2010). Towards a model public sector integrity commission. *Australian Journal of Public Administration, 69*(3), 251–262.

Prenzler, T., Mihinjac, M., & Porter, L. (2013). Reconciling stakeholder interests in police complaints and discipline systems. *Police Practice and Research: An International Journal, 14*(2), 155–168.

Prenzler, T. (2009a). *Ethics and accountability in criminal justice.* Brisbane: Australian Academic Press.

Prenzler, T. (2009b). *Preventing burglary in commercial and institutional settings: a place management and partnerships approach.* Washington: ASIS Foundation.

Prenzler, T. (2011). The evolution of police oversight in Australia. *Policing and Society, 21*(3), 284–303.

Quah, J. S. T. (2003). *Curbing corruption in Asia: a comparative study of six countries.* Singapore: Marshall Cavendish Academic.

Quah, J. S. T. (2010). Defying institutional failure: learning from the experiences of anti-corruption agencies in four Asian countries. *Crime Law and Social Change, 53*(1), 23–54.

Recanatini, F. (2011). Assessing corruption at the country level. In A. Graycar & R. G. Smith (Eds.), *Handbook of global research and practice in corruption* (pp. 34–62). Cheltenham, UK: Edward Elgar.

Roman, J., Walsh, K., Lachman, P., & Yahner, J. (2012). *Post-conviction DNA testing and wrongful conviction.* Washington: Urban Institute.

Rose-Ackerman, S. (1999). *Corruption and government: causes, consequences and reform.* Cambridge: Cambridge University Press.

Ross, Y. (2005). *Ethics in law: lawyers' responsibility and accountability in Australia.* Sydney: LexisNexis Butterworths.

Rozenberg, J. (1992). Miscarriages of justice. In E. Stockdale & S. Cassales (Eds.), *Criminal justice under stress* (pp. 91–116). London: Blackstone.

Russell, J. (2007). *Terrorism pre-charge detention comparative law study.* London: Liberty.

Salter, M. (2010). *Lawful but corrupt: gaming and the problem of institutional corruption in the private sector.* Harvard Business School, http://papers.ssrn.com/sol3/papers.cfm?abstract_id=1726004

Salusinszky, I. (12 Mar 2009). Watchdog's tale, *The Australian*, p. 11.

Savedoff, W. D. (2007). *The impact of information and accountability on hospital procurement corruption in Argentina and Bolivia.* Portland, ME: Social Insight.

Scott, I. (2011a). The Hong Kong ICAC's approach to corruption control. In A. Graycar & R. Smith (Eds.), *Handbook of global research and practice in corruption* Cheltenham, UK: Edward Elgar.

Scott, I. (2011b). The Hong Kong ICAC's approach to corruption control. In Adam Graycar & Russell G. Smith (Eds.), *Handbook of global research and practice in corruption* (pp. 401–415). Cheltenham, UK: Edward Elgar.

Sparrow, M. (2000a). *License to steal: how fraud bleeds America's health care system*. Boulder: Westview Press.

Sparrow, M. (2000b). *The regulatory craft: controlling risks, solving problems compliance, and managing compliance*. Washington: Brookings Institution Press.

Taylor, P. (7 Oct 2009). Publlic sector needs watching, *The Australian*, 2.

Terrall, B. (2008, January 30). Suharto's legacy lives on through the military. *South China Morning Post*, p. 13.

Toch, H. (2012). *Cop watch: Spectators, social media, and police reform*. Washington, DC: American Psychological Association.

Transparency International (2000). *TI source book 2000: confronting corruption: the elements of a National Integrity System*. Retrieved 17 January 2013, from http://archive.transparency.org/publications/sourcebook

Transparency International (2001). *Global corruption report 2001*. Berlin, Transparency International, http://www.transparency.org/whatwedo/pub/global_corruption_report_2001

Transparency International (2006). *Handbook for curbing corruption in public procurement*. Berlin, Transparency International, http://www.transparency.org/whatwedo/pub/handbook_for_curbing_corruption_in_public_procurement

Transparency International (2007). *Global corruption report*. Cambridge, Cambridge University Press, http://www.cambridge.org/knowledge/isbn/item1164278/Global%20Corruption%20Report%202007

Transparency International (2010). *CPI long methodological brief*. http://transparency.ee/cm/files/cpi2010_long_methodology_en.pdf

Transparency International (2011). *Global corruption barometer 2010/11*. http://gcb.transparency.org/gcb201011/in_detail/

Transparency International (2012). *Corruption perception index 2012*. Berlin, Transparency International, http://cpi.transparency.org/cpi2012/

10.1057/9781137335098

Transparency International (2013). *National Integrity System background rationale and methodology.* Retrieved 17 January 2013, from http://www.transparency.org/files/content/nis/NationalIntegritySystem_Background_and_Methodology.pdf

Tuttle, B. R. (2009). *How Newark became Newark : the rise, fall, and rebirth of an American city.* New Brunswick, NJ: Rivergate Books.

U4 (2010). *International good practice in anti-corruption legislation.* Bergen, U4 Anti-Corruption Resource Centre, http://www.u4.no/publications/international-good-practice-in-anti-corruption-legislation/

United Nations Convention Against Corruption (2004), UN Office on Drugs and Crime (2004). http://www.unodc.org/unodc/en/treaties/CAC/

USAID (2009). *Anticorruption assessment handbook.* Washington, United States Agency for International Development, http://transition.usaid.gov/our_work/democracy_and_governance/technical_areas/anticorruption_handbook/Handbook_2009.pdf

US Congress Senate (1974). *Select Committee on Presidential Campaign Activities.* Washington, DC.

Uslaner, E. M. (2008). *Corruption, inequality, and the rule of law.* Cambridge: Cambridge University Press.

Walker, C., & McCartney, C. (2008). Criminal justice and miscarriages of justice in England and Wales. In C. Huff & M. Killias (Eds.), *Wrongful conviction: international perspectives on miscarriages of justice* (pp. 183–211). Philadelphia: Temple University Press.

Wanna, J ., & Arklay, T. (2010). *The Ayes have it: the history of the Queensland Parliament 1957–1989.* Canberra: ANU E-Press.

Ware, G .T., Moss, S., Edgardo Campos, J., & Noon, G. P. (2011). Corruption in procurement. In A. Graycar & R. G. Smith (Eds.), *Handbook of global research and practice in corruption.* Cheltenham, UK: Edward Elgar.

World Bank (2007). *Stolen Asset Recovery (StAR) Initiative: Challenges, opportunities, and action Plan.* Washington, DC.

World Bank (2012). *Worldwide governance indicators.* Washington, World Bank, 26 Feb 2012, http://info.worldbank.org/governance/wgi/scchart.asp

World Economic Forum (2013). *Global Agenda Council on Anti-Corruption & Transparency 2013.* Retrieved September 16, 2013, from

10.1057/9781137335098

http://www.weforum.org/content/global-agenda-council-anti-corruption-transparency-2013.

Wortley, R. (2002). *Situational prison control: crime prevention in correctional institutions*. Cambridge: Cambridge University Press.

Wrong, M. (2009). *It's our turn to eat: the story of a Kenyan whistle-blower*. New York: HarperCollins Publishing.

Yakovlev, E. & Zhuravskaya, E. (2006). *State capture: from Yeltsin to Putin*. CEFIR / NES Working Paper series Working Paper No 94, Centre for Economic and Financial Research at New Economic School, http://www.cefir.ru/ezhuravskaya/research/Yakovlev_Zhuravskaya_Capture_Yeltsin_Putin.pdf

10.1057/9781137335098

Index

Aboriginal Land Council
    custodians, 130–1
Abramoff, Jack, 14–15
abuse of discretion, 8
abuse of public office, 51
activities, where corruption
    occurs, 10–11
ADB-OECD Anti-Corruption
    Initiative, 67
Africa, 21
African Union Convention, 67
Alemán, Arnoldo, 13
Anti-Bribery Convention, 37
anti-corruption agencies
    (ACAs), 51–6, 81–3, 141
anti-corruption measures,
    50–69
    anti-corruption agencies,
        51–6, 81–3, 141
    civil society, 67–9
    crime prevention, 70–85
    integrity pacts, 109–10
    integrity systems, 56–60,
        81–3
    international efforts,
        60–7, 143
    universal model for, 83–5
appeals systems, 98–9
Arab Spring, 13
Argentina, 123–6
Asia-Pacific Economic
    Cooperation (APEC), 67
Asia Pacific Group on Money
    Laundering, 67
asset recovery, 63–4

audits, 56–7
Australia, 26, 38–42, 51, 52, 58,
    81–3, 98, 103, 141
authority systems, 19–20

behaviour, 35
bid rigging, 105–6
Birch, Sarah, 56
Birmingham Six case, 93
Blagojevich, Rod, 9
Boeing, 102
Bolivia, 119–20, 123
Boston Gun Project, 75
Braithwaite, J., 75
Bribe Payers Index, 46–7
bribery, 3–5, 10, 14, 22, 27, 28,
    51, 117, 131
Bribery Act 2010, 51
bureaucracy, 20

Cammarano, Peter, 132
campaign financing, 14
cartels, 25
Chile, 122–3
China, 22, 80–1
Ciavarella, Mark, 27–8
civil society, 67–9
Claes, Willy, 101
clans, 24
Clarke, R.V., 70–1, 72
code of ethics, 57–8
Coeme, Guy, 101
coercion, 5
collusion, 29, 31
Comalco, 26, 27

10.1057/9781137335098

Commonwealth Criminal Code, 51
Conahan, Michael T., 27–8
conflict of interest, 6–8, 30–1, 118
contract manipulation, 6
controlling facilitators, 77
corruption
    controlling, 31
    costs of, 3, 44–5
    in cultural context, 19–21
    definitions of, 10
    drivers of, 15
    examples of, 26–8
    harm from, 23–4
    location of, 15–17
    measuring, 33–49
    occurrence of, 10–12
    perception of, 35
    in political context, 24–6
    reasons for, 28–32
    risk for, 37–8
    scale of, 12–15
    types of, 3–9
    understanding, 18–32
corruption control, *see* anti-corruption
        measures
Corruption Perception Index (CPI), 35,
        45–6, 48
corruption prevention
    see also anti-corruption measures
    in criminal justice, 87–99
    innovations in, 109–10
    in public health, 114–26
    in public sector procurement, 100–13
    in urban planning, 127–43
Corruption Vulnerability Assessments
        (CVAs), 110
Costa Rica, 119
Council of Europe, 66
Country Diagnostic Surveys, 48
crime prevention, 70–85, 142
Criminal Cases Review Commission
        (CCRC), 98–9
criminalization, 63
criminal justice systems
    corruption in, 88–90
    corruption prevention in, 87–99

guardianship and regulation, 97–9
measures of corruption in,
        90–1
miscarriages of justice, 91–3, 97–9
opportunity factors, 93–4
reducing opportunity in, 95–7
cronyism, 9
cultural context, 19–21

data-matching, 76
death penalty, 92
Department of Investigation (DOI),
        37, 53
de Sousa, Luis, 51, 55
discretion, abuse of, 8
DNA testing, 96
donor funds, 118
Doo-hwan, Chun, 13
drug companies, 117–18
drug counterfeiting, 118
Druyan, Darleen, 102

education, 43
Egypt, 13
elections, 56
electoral corruption, 56
elite cartels, 25
embezzlement, 5–6, 51
enforcement pyramid, 75
England, 26
enhanced due diligence, 110
Enron, 7
entry screening, 77
e-procurement, 110
ethical codes, 57–8
ethical interviewing, 95
Etzioni, Amitai, 25–6
events, 17
exclusionary rule, 77
extortion, 5, 10, 14, 116

fake drugs, 118
favouritism, 41
Felson, Marcus, 19, 20
Financial Action Task Force
        (FATF), 67

Financial Management and
    Accountability Act, 1997, 51
Finland, 25
first-generation measurement tools,
    35, 36
forensic evidence, 94, 98
Foster, Ken, 130
fraud, 5–6

G20, 66–7
Gaddafi, Muammar, 12–13
game the system, 25
gaming, 14
gift giving, 21–3, 103, 117
Global Corruption Barometer, 36, 46,
    47, 90–1, 116
global financial crisis, 7
Global Integrity Index, 36
Global Witness, 68
Gorta, Angela, 35, 37–8, 59
Governance and Corruption
    Diagnostic Survey, 46
governance capacity, loss of, 23–4
grand corruption, 12–13
greed, 15
guanxi, 22
guardianship, 97–9, 133–4
Guildford Four case, 93

health systems,*see* public health
high-risk functions, 37–8
Hong Kong, Independent Commission
    against Corruption (ICAC), 41–2,
    52, 54, 79–81, 84, 98

Independent Commission against
    Corruption (ICAC), 41–2, 52, 54,
    79–81, 84, 98
individuals, 15, 17, 29
Indonesia, 12, 111–12
inequality trap, 20–1
influence markets, 25
influence peddling, 9, 26, 51
institutions, 20–1
integrity, 31, 32
integrity commissions, 81–3

integrity framework, 59
integrity pacts, 109–10
integrity systems, 56–60, 83–4
Inter-American Convention against
    Corruption of the Organization of
    American States, 67
international co-operation, 63
International Crime Victims Survey,
    36, 46
Irish Republican Army (IRA), 92
Italy, 17

James, Sharpe, 132
Johnston, Michael, 24

Kenya, 55
Kickback Brokers scheme, 105
Klitgaard, Robert, 22, 23
Krastev, Ivan, 48
Kuhlhorn, E., 72

Lambsdorff, Johann Graf, 45
Latin America, 115, 119–26
Lessig, Lawrence, 14
Leveson Inquiry, 90
Libya, 12–13
lobbying, 13–15
Local Aboriginal Land Council
    (LALC), 130–1

Mack, Tony, 131–2
Maguire Seven case, 93
Malaysia, 52, 111
Marcos, Ferdinand, 12
Mason, Vanessa, 130
Mauss, Marcel, 21
measures of corruption, 33–49
    costs of corruption, 44–5
    in criminal justice systems, 90–1
    extent of corruption, 38–44
    risk for, 37–8
    tools for, 35–7
medical litigation, 118
milk subsidies, 27
misappropriation, 5–6, 14, 51
miscarriages of justice, 91–3, 97–9

modern societies, 20
mortgage-backed securities, 7
Mubarak, Hosni, 13
Mungiu-Pippidi, Alina, 65, 69

national integrity system, 32, 56–60
need, 15
nepotism, 8–9, 14
Netherlands, 40
New Jersey, 131–2
New York City, 37, 52–3
Nicaragua, 13
Nixon, Richard, 27
non-governmental organizations
    (NGOs), 68, 71, 141
NSW Independent Commission against
    Corruption (ICAC NSW), 16
Nye, Joseph, 23

Obama, Barack, 9
OECD Convention on Combating
    Bribery of Foreign Public
    Officials in International Business
    Transactions, 65–6
OECD countries, 58–9
official moguls, 24
oligarchs, 24
Olken, Benjamin, 44–5
ombudsman, 57
Open Budget Index, 36
opportunities
    for corruption, 28–9
    in criminal justice systems, 93–4
    in public sector procurement, 103–6
    reducing, 78, 95–7
organizations, 15–16, 17, 57
Oxford Policy Management, 44

Paraguay, 12
patrimonial societies, 19, 20
patronage, 8, 9
pay to play, 9
perception, of corruption, 35
performance audits, 56–7
perjury, 94
petty corruption, 12, 13

pharmaceuticals, 117–18
Philippines, 12
places, where corruption occurs,
    11–12, 128
Police and Criminal Evidence Act
    (PACE), 97
police corruption, 87–99
political context, 24–6
political institutions, 20–1
politicians, 7, 9, 13, 26, 27, 30–1
Pope, Jeremy, 32
prisons, 96
professional practice standards, 57–8
Public Expenditure and Financial
    Accountability Framework
    (PEFA), 36
public health
    case studies, 119–20, 123–6
    influences of corrupt practices in,
        120–1
    intervention impact studies, 122–4
    in Latin America, 115, 119–26
    nature and extent of corruption in,
        115–18
    preventing corruption in, 114–26
public policy, 27, 28
public sector procurement, 100–13
    bid rigging, 105–6
    case studies, 111–13
    dimensions, impacts, and cases of
        corruption in, 101–2
    e-procurement, 110
    grey areas, 102–3, 107
    modi operandi and opportunity,
        103–5
    preventing corruption in, 106–8,
        109–10
    types of, 105–6
    warning flags, 108–9
Pyo Family Trust, 131

Quah, John, 53–4

RailCorp, 16
rational-legal system, 20
Recanatini, Francesca, 42

regulation, of criminal justice systems, 97–9
regulatory capture, 118
regulatory failure, 74
regulatory theory, 70–85
rent seeking, 21–3
rezoning processes, 128–9
risk assessments, 110
risk mitigation, 59–60
Rose-Ackerman, Susan, 22–3
rule-making game, 14
rule setting, 77
Russia, 13

Salter, Malcolm, 14
Sanhueza, Christian, 102
Sears, Michael M., 102
second-generation measurement tools, 35–6
sectors, where corruption occurs, 11
Seko, Mobutu Sese, 12
self-dealing, 6
sentencing guidelines, 95
Shui-Ban, Chen, 13
Siemens, 16
Singapore, 51, 53–4
situational corruption, 29
situational crime prevention (SCP), 71–9, 142
situational prevention, 26
societies
    corrupt, 15, 16–17
    modern, 20
    patrimonial, 19, 20
    traditional, 19, 20
South Korea, 13, 54
standards of conduct, 57–8
state capture, 13–14
Stroessner, Alfredo, 12
structural corruption, 29, 30–1
Suharto, President, 12
surveillance, 77

Tae-woo, Roh, 13
Taiwan, 13

target hardening, 77
Taylor, Clive, 102
Thailand, 54
theft, 5–6, 10
third-generation measurement tools, 36–7
toxic securities, 7
trading in influence, 9, 51
traditional societies, 19, 20
transitional economies, 13
Transparency International, 32, 101, 111–12
    Corruption Perception Index (CPI), 35, 45–6, 48
    Global Corruption Barometer, 36, 46, 47, 90–1, 116
Transue, Hilary, 28
Tunisia, 13
Types, Activities, Sectors, Places (TASP), 10–12, 36, 40, 89, 142

U4, 68
United Kingdom, 51, 90, 92–3, 98–9, 118
United Nations Convention Against Corruption (UNCAC), 10, 37, 61–5, 84
United States, 27–8, 131–2
United States Death Penalty Information Center, 92
Universal Declaration of Human Rights, 65
urban planning
    Aboriginal Land Council custodians, 130–1
    case studies, 130–2
    preventing corruption in, 127–43
    Wollongong Council, 129–30, 134–9
USAID Agency, 42
Uslaner, Eric, 20–1

Ward, Judith, 93
Weber, Max, 19, 20
Wollongong Council, 129–30, 134–9
work environment, corruption in, 41

World Bank, 3, 36, 42, 44,
48, 80
World Bank Governance Indicators
(WBGI), 35, 46, 47–8
World Economics Forum, 3

Worldwide Governance Indicators, 46,
47–8
Wrong, Michela, 55

Zaire, 12

10.1057/9781137335098

CPSIA information can be obtained at www.ICGtesting.com
Printed in the USA
LVOW07*0816011214

416417LV00007B/123/P